ISBN 978-1-330-32086-0
PIBN 10026317

# 1 MONTH OF
# FREE
# READING

## at
## www.ForgottenBooks.com

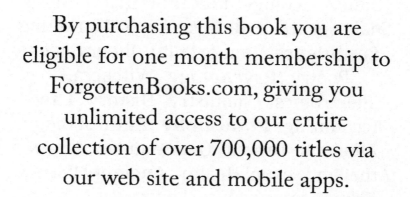

By purchasing this book you are eligible for one month membership to ForgottenBooks.com, giving you unlimited access to our entire collection of over 700,000 titles via our web site and mobile apps.

To claim your free month visit:
www.forgottenbooks.com/free26317

English
Français
Deutsche
Italiano
Español
Português

# www.forgottenbooks.com

**Mythology** Photography **Fiction**
Fishing Christianity **Art** Cooking
Essays Buddhism Freemasonry
Medicine **Biology** Music **Ancient
Egypt** Evolution Carpentry Physics
Dance Geology **Mathematics** Fitness
Shakespeare **Folklore** Yoga Marketing
**Confidence** Immortality Biographies
Poetry **Psychology** Witchcraft
Electronics Chemistry History **Law**
Accounting **Philosophy** Anthropology
Alchemy Drama Quantum Mechanics
Atheism Sexual Health **Ancient History**
**Entrepreneurship** Languages Sport
Paleontology Needlework Islam
**Metaphysics** Investment Archaeology
Parenting Statistics Criminology
**Motivational**

# VITTORIA COLONNA

## A Study

*WITH TRANSLATIONS OF SOME OF HER PUBLISHED*

*AND UNPUBLISHED SONNETS*

BY THE

### Hon. ALETHEA LAWLEY

SECOND EDITION, REVISED

LONDON

GILBERT & RIVINGTON,

*Limited*

ST. JOHN'S HOUSE, CLERKENWELL ROAD, E.C.

1889

LONDON:
PRINTED BY GILBERT AND RIVINGTON, LD,
ST. JOHN'S HOUSE, CLERKENWELL ROAD. E.C.

# PREFACE.

THERE is no claim in the following pages to present more than a sketch of Vittoria Colonna's life. Her history is veiled in an obscurity which prevents great minuteness of detail, and which conceals many of the hidden particulars which form the charm of biography.

In order to cast some light upon this subject, and to give personality to this sketch, I have for the most part selected for translation into English, those of Vittoria's sonnets which refer to the leading events of her life, and reflect in some degree her own thoughts and words on these occasions.

The attempt to translate these sonnets is difficult under two aspects : in the first place there is only one commentator on Vittoria's poems, Rinaldo Corso ; and whenever an intricate or complicated passage occurs in the sonnet of which he is treating, he has no hesitation in omitting the entire passage, and passes on to subjects which are clear and straightforward. From him no help can be looked for or obtained. The other difficulty lies in the obscurity of many of the sonnets in the original. The fact that Vittoria's works were printed without her knowledge or sanction, brought with it the disadvantage of their being published without the corrections and alterations that the authoress alone could give. The result is one which complicates the difficulties for a translator in every way; and I must here acknowledge with grateful thanks the help I have received in this work of translation from a friend. Whatever merit there is in these translations is due to him; his suggestions and alterations having given to my efforts whatever claim they may have to poetic rendering.

I must also express my thanks to Mr. John Addington Symonds, for the generous permission given me to make use of his beautiful translations of Michelangelo's sonnets to Vittoria Colonna.

The sonnets at pages 8 and 47 are by

another friend, to whose advice and encouragement, throughout the whole of my work, I am deeply indebted.

I have been unable to discover the author of the sonnet on pages 96, 97.

The kindness and courtesy I have met with in Italy will ever remain in my memory. To Barone B. Podestà, and Signor Martinelli at the Magliabecchiana Library in Florence, and to Conte Camillo Soranzo, and Professore Signor Taddeo Wiel at the Marciana Library, in Venice, my warmest thanks are due for the unfailing assistance I have received from them, and the kindly readiness with which they have always helped me in my researches.

I have adhered generally to the foreign renderings of titles; the English equivalents, being different, would be apt to give a mistaken impression.

The sources from which I have collected most of the material for the following work are: Le Rime di Vittoria Colonna, corretti su i testi a penna e publicate con la vita della medesima ec. Roma, 1840, by Cav. Pietro Visconti: Le Rime de Vittoria Colonna, Marchesana di Pescara; colla vita della medesima; scritta da Giovanni Battista Rota; Bergamo, 1760: Rime e Letere di Vittoria Colonna, Marchesana di Pescara; di G. Enrico Saltini; Firenze, 1860.

The disputes and discussions as to an authentic portrait of Vittoria Colonna are too well known to need comment. The picture of her in the Colonna Gallery at Rome, from which the frontispiece in this book is taken, is, however, generally accepted as a true representation of her. It is a three-quarter picture, said to be by Muziano,[1] and the likeness is that of a beautiful woman of about twenty-eight or thirty years of age. The hair grows in a peak on the forehead, and is of a bright auburn colour; and the poet Galeazzo di Tarsia,[2] who, in the fashion of the

[1] Girolamo Muziano, born at Acquafredda, near Brescia, in 152?, would have been too young to have painted the original; and Trollope, in his " Decade of Italian Women," speaking of this portrait, says : " It is supposed to be a copy by Girolamo Muziano from an original picture of some artist of higher note."

[2] Rime di Galeazzo di Tarsia, Edizione Napolitano, 1758 Sonetto 33, e Sonetto 4.

day, professed himself her devoted slave and fervent admirer and adorer, speaks of it more than once, when singing the praises of his lady, as the—

> "Trecce d' or che in gli altri giri
>    Non è ch' unqua pareggi o sole o stella ;"

while in another place he declares that the sun and his lady resemble each other : " Both with golden locks lucid and shining" ("Ambi con chiome d' or lucide e terse"). The portrait gives the impression of great beauty. The face is small, with a thoughtful, grave expression. The eyes and eye-brows are dark brown ; while on her head she wears a white coif fastened by a jewelled band. The forehead is beautifully shaped and developed, and the whole bearing calm and dignified.

FLORENCE, 1888.

# VITTORIA COLONNA.

## I.

IN the fourteenth century, a castle standing on the lower ridge of the mountains of Albano was the cause of as much vexation and toil to the Romans of that day, as they had experienced of old on the opposite height of Tusculum. Three great Roman families, the Colonna, the Orsini, and the Savelli, had divided among themselves the lovely group of these Alban hills, from whence not only did they swoop down on the neighbouring towns and cities, but could also close the passes to the south, and so secure to themselves undisturbed possession of the surrounding country.

The castle of Marino was the key to one of these passes, and was the scene of strife between Cola di Rienzi[1] and the Orsini, when the castle was held by this family. More con-

[1] Rienzi, born about 1310, was assassinated in 1354.

tests occurred here in the end of the fourteenth, and beginning of the fifteenth centuries, during the confusion arising from two claimants disputing the papal throne  But when at the Council of Constance (1417), Oddo Colonna was elected Pope as Martin V., and a reign of peace was inaugurated, Marino passed into the possession of the Colonna, in whose hands it is at this day; the eldest son of this noble family taking from it the title of Duke of Marino.

In this castle was born in 1490 Vittoria, the youngest daughter of Fabrizio Colonna, Seignior of Paliano, and afterwards Prince of Tagliacozzo.  He was descended from a brother of Pope Martin V., and was destined by his family for the Church, but his own tastes being firmly fixed on a military career, he escaped from his father's house, and took part in the crusade against the Turks at Otranto in 1481. His wife was Agnese di Montefeltro, youngest daughter of Federigo, Duke of Urbino.[2]

---

[2] Those of my readers who are familiar with the Uffizi

At the age of five, Vittoria was affianced to Ferrante Francesco d'Avalos, Marchese di Pescara. Their betrothal was the suggestion of Ferrante II., King of Sicily and Naples, who desired by such an alliance to unite in ties of family relationship the powerful house of Colonna with one of the chief Spanish families then settled in Italy, and so secure more firmly to his cause the somewhat vacillating allegiance of these haughty Barons.

The following sonnet by Vittoria, written after her husband's death, alludes to this early betrothal :—

[3] To perfect growth my spirit scarce had gained,
When Heaven, prescribing every aim beside,
With one high being gave me to abide,
And by his light be nurtured and sustained.

---

Gallery at Florence will remember the portraits of Duke Federigo of Urbino and his wife Battista Sforza, by Pietro della Francesca, enclosed in one frame, and facing each other in profile.

[3] S'appena avean gli spirti intera vita,
    Quando il ciel gli prescrisse ogn' altro oggetto
    E sol m' apparve il bel celeste aspetto,
    Della cui luce io fui sempre nodrita ;

What fell decree hath since my soul constrained
To quit its loved retreat, its refuge tried,
Hath light, and day, and intercourse denied,
And blind confusion to my path ordained?

When Heaven and Nature of one mind were led
To join our lives, what envious hand hath known,
What daring foe, to separate the tie?
If this frail body by his life was fed,
Was born for him, was his, his very own,
Then when he died 'twas time for me to die

Don Ferrante d'Avalos, Marchese di Pescara,
was born near Toledo, in the province of Old
Castile, of a family unable to boast of any illus-
trious member, though of old and noble descent.
Pescara's father died young, leaving this only
child. Of his mother little is known, beyond

---

Qual dura legge ha poi l' alma sbandita
   Dal grato albergo anzi divin ricetto?
   La scorta, il lume, 'l giorno l' è interdetto;
   Onde cammina in cieco error smarrita.

Se la natura e'l ciel con pari voglia
   Ne legò insieme, ahi qual invido ardire
   Quale inimica forza ne disciolse!
Se'l viver suo nodrì mia frale spoglia,
   Per lui nacqui, ero sua, per sè mi tolse;
   Nella sua morte ancor dovea morire.

the fact that she belonged to an honourable
Sicilian family.   There is a quaint description
in Giovanni Filocalo's " Life of the Marquis of
Pescara," of the reception given to Ferdinand of
Spam, on the occasion of his visiting Naples to
remove Gonsalvo di Cordova, whom he sus-
pected of ambitious designs in regard of that
fair domain.   " After the feast had been served,
the tables being removed, dancing began ;
among the dancers was the young Pescara,
who with such art and such gravity made
numerous steps, and fulfilled all the varieties
of the dance, that even the King, a man of
extremest prudence and judgment, having fixed
his eyes solely on him, said publicly to the
Barons, while pointing out to them Pescara :
' That youth, from his movements and appear-
ance, seems to me a captain greater than those
around him, and, if my opinion errs not, he will
prosper above them all.'   The youth, far from
being conceited by the judgment passed on him
by so great a King, replied that his Majesty had
wished to put too heavy a weight on his youth-
ful shoulders, for that he would have much to

sweat in war and in peace in order to merit
this encomium which the King, from the super-
abundance of his goodwill towards him, had
placed on him."

Upon the return of King Ferdinand to Spain,
Pescara retired to his lands, where he led the
life of a country gentleman, and occupied him-
self in magisterial duties, settling the disputes
of his neighbours, equals, and inferiors alike,
and gaining a high reputation for equity and
moderation.

The conditions for the marriage settlements
of Vittoria Colonna and Ferrante d'Avalos
were signed at Marino in 1507; but, as often
happened at that time, an interval of two years
occurred before the marriage took place at
Ischia.  Vittoria's beauty, of no common order,
was matched by great powers of mind, and
though little is known of her earlier years,[4] we

---

[4] Reumont, one of the most minute of her biographers,
in his "Vittoria Colonna, Leben, Dichten, Glauben in
XVI. Jahrhundert," says, "We know nothing about
Vittoria's childhood" ("Wir wissen nichts über Vittoria's
Kindheit").

can imagine that, like most high-born Italian ladies, she was brought up at some convent under the patronage of her family. We can see by her poems and writings that her education had been careful and judicious, and that she had been trained in the fine arts, and Latin, as well as the classical lore of her own tongue. Her betrothed husband was a bridegroom worthy of her; he shared her love of literature, was handsome, valiant, and endowed with qualities which were to rank him among the first generals of the age.

The wedding was celebrated on the 27th of December, 1509, and was almost royal in its magnificence and gorgeousness. The chroniclers of the day agree in asserting that nowhere could be found a more beautiful, virtuous, or highly gifted couple than Vittoria Colonna and Ferrante d'Avalos. They were both nineteen years of age when the marriage took place. To Vittoria the sorrow of leaving her home was a keen one; and she felt especially the separation from her eldest brother Federigo. He died in 1516, and two beautiful sonnets, written by her to his memory, show how strong was her love for him.   We give one of them here :—

[5] Clear soul, by what a swift, enlargèd flight,
　Strong and direct, thou hast the skies attained,
　Through clouds obscure,which on the earth remained,
　How welcome none can say, how pure, how bright !
　In vesture of such substance woven aright,
　Thy mortal shape so well its guest contained,
　Till in frail home no longer entertained,
　Outshone for thee at once celestial light.

My Frederic blest, now are the bonds untied
Of kinship close, now strained the subtle chain
Which bound us both to fare the better way.

---

[5] Anima chiara, or pur larga e spedita
　　Strada prendesti al ciel da questa oscura
　　Valle mondana, in su volando pura,
　　Più ch'io non posso dir, bella e gradita !
　Era di ricco stame intorno ordita
　　La tua veste mortal con tal misura,
　　Che 'l fin di questa tua fragil figura
　　Ti fu principio all' altra miglior vita.

　Beato Federigo, or son disciolti
　　I legami del sangue, e quel più caro
　　Nodo è ristretto ch'a ben far mi spinse.

Fain would I hear, but patient must I bide,
How thou from God high graces could obtain
Most sweetly to accept the bitter day.      (R. S. P.)

Pescara and his bride went first to Naples, where numerous feasts and entertainments were held in honour of the newly married pair. From there they removed to Pietralba, a villa belonging to the d'Avalos family, on the borders of Monte Ermo; but their permanent home was the lovely island of Ischia, the feudal stronghold of the Pescara. Constance d'Avalos, Duchessa di Francavilla, in her capacity of perpetual chatelaine of the island, was living there, and Vittoria found in her a congenial and elevating companion. She was aunt to Pescara;[6] a woman of iron will and energies, and held in high repute, both for her powers as ruler, and for her knowledge and love of letters. Many of Vittoria's happiest days were passed here,

---

Or convien ch'io riguardi e non ch'io ascolti
Da te le grazie onde il Signor ti strinse
A ricever più dolce il giorno amaro.

[6] She was sister of Alfonso, Marchese di Pescara, whose titles and estates had descended to Vittoria's husband.

uniting the joys of wedded life with an earnest
pursuit of her loved studies, and for three years
nothing occurred to disturb what might be
called an uninterrupted honeymoon.

This calm was not to last. Pescara, attracted
by the sounds of war, hastened to assist the
cause of his liege lord, Ferdinand the Catholic,
against Louis XII. of France.

Louis XII. had invaded Italy a few years
previously, to make good his pretensions to the
Duchy of Milan, through his grandmother,
Valentina Visconti. She was the daughter of
Gian Galeazzo Visconti and Isabella of France,
and in 1389 had married Louis, Duke of Or-
leans. Her marriage portion was the lordship
of Asti, and a right to the Duchy of Milan,
should the male branch of the Visconti become
extinct. She had two brothers, Giovanni, and
Filippo. Maria, both of whom died without
male issue. Filippo left, however, an illegiti-
mate daughter, Bianca, married to Francesco
Sforza, who, on the death of Filippo, claimed
and obtained the duchy in right of his wife.
It was to dispossess the Sforza that Louis

urged his claim, through the superior right, as he held it, of his grandmother.

The war now commencing, and known in history as that of "the Holy League," was brought about by Pope Julius II. (della Rovere). Having gained all he could look for from the alliance he had formed at Cambray (1508) with Louis XII., he was eager to withdraw from his French ally, and turn to a quarter where his policy suggested greater advantages to be obtained. He induced Spain and Venice to espouse his cause, and operations were at once commenced by the Spaniards for besieging Bologna. Louis despatched his army into Italy, under the command of his nephew, Gaston de Foix, Duc de Nemours, who made a sudden and brilliant march to the relief of the besieged town.

Vittoria's father had been appointed Governor-General of the united Italian and Spanish forces, and Pescara joined him with a company of armed followers, levied at his own cost, and equipped, according to Giovio,[7] in most splendid

---

[7] Paolo Giovio was born at Como in 1483, and died at

accoutrements. The Marchese was appointed Captain-General of the light cavalry, a post of much honour for so young a commander.

To Vittoria the trial of separation from her husband was great. But she never allowed her love to interfere with duty. On the contrary, she used her influence to encourage and con-firm his ardour, and urged him to prove himself in every way worthy of his heroic ancestors. To both of them the chivalrous mind of the times did much, no doubt, to soften the pain of parting, for at this moment all Europe was filled with high and romantic ideas of chivalry, and Ferrante d'Avalos was in no way behind his age. He was high-souled, noble, and generous; and the injunction of the Spartan mother to her son, " Or with this, or upon it," " O con questo, o su questo," was the motto he bore on his shield. He left Ischia early in 1512

---

Florence in 1552. He lost all his pos-essions in the sack of Rome in 1527, but was made Bishop of Nocera by Clement VII., amassed great wealth, and built for himself a sumptuous villa on the shores of the Lake of Como, on the site where Pliny the Younger's villa had stood.

with Raimondo di Cardona,[8] Viceroy of Naples, who was also on his way to join the forces of Spain, together with the chief nobles of the land. Vittoria bravely restrained her tears during the sad moments of farewell ; and it was not till her husband was gone, and the knowledge of her solitude came home to her, that she broke down.

During the lonely days that followed Pescara's departure, Vittoria rarely left the house, her time being engrossed in close study, and in writing, though her chief occupation was the education of Alfonso d'Avalos, the young Marchese del Vasto, her husband's nearest relation.[9] The boy, extremely handsome, was of a wild and ungovernable temper, and Vittoria had no easy task before her in attempting to smooth and curb a nature that resented interference or discipline. By her tact and gentleness she

---

[8] Raimondo di Cardona's name has come down to us with the imputation of coward attached to it. He is said to have taken flight at the battle of Ravenna, " being a man of small courage," and Julius II., knowing this accusation, was wont to call him " Madame di Cardona."

[9] Their fathers having been brothers, they were first cousins.

succeeded in softening and changing her young kinsman.  She instilled into him some of her own taste for letters, and raised in him a love for higher things than mere sports and athletics, which at one time had been his only interest.

Vittoria's anxiety as to her husband was allayed to some extent by her hearing that on his arrival at the camp he had been appointed to the high command of Captain-General of Cavalry; a position to which he could hardly have hoped to aspire, considering he was then only twenty-one years of age.

But her joy was soon turned into mourning when the news of the disastrous battle of Ravenna reached her ears.  Here, on Easter Sunday, 11th of April, 1512, the two armies— the French, and the allied Italians and Spaniards —met face to face.

An obstinate and bloody fight ensued, in which the French ultimately remained con- querors, though they lost their general, Gaston de Foix.[1]  The success of the French has been

---

[1] He fell, covered with wounds, on the field of battle, at

ascribed to the malice of the Spaniards, whose intention, it is said, was to sacrifice their Italian allies, in order that they might reap the whole glory of the victory. Fabrizio Colonna, perceiving this, threw himself boldly into the front rank of the enemy, and opened the fight. If he had delayed longer all his countrymen would have been shot down by the enemy's artillery. Overcome by numbers, and sorely wounded, he was taken prisoner, and gave himself up to Alfonso d'Este, Duke of Ferrara,[2] in order not to surrender to the French, to whom he bore a special hatred. Later in the day the same fate befell his son-in-law Pescara, who was taken prisoner, after giving signal proofs of valour, and when so grievously wounded that all further resistance was vain. Both he and Fabrizio were taken to Milan, and entrusted to the care of Gian Giacomo Trivulzio, Pescara's maternal

---

the very moment of victory, in the twenty-third year of his age, and was buried at Milan with such pomp and state that the ceremony was more like a triumph than a funeral.

[2] Alfonso favoured the French cause.

uncle; while a special messenger was despatched to Vittoria to apprise her of the fate that had befallen her father and husband. Fabrizio's position was soon altered from that of a prisoner to a mediator, for the French, having retired from Italy after the Battle of Ravenna, Alfonso, Duke of Ferrara, who had espoused their cause, was desirous of making his peace with the Pope. Fabrizio offered his services as peacemaker, for which intent the Duke gave him his liberty, and they went together to Rome. They failed, however, in accomplishing this purpose, and Fabrizio so far fell under Julius's displeasure as to incur sentence of excommunication.

Pescara remained a prisoner in his uncle's house in Milan, and employed his leisure hours in inscribing to his wife a "Dialogue of Love," which unfortunately has not come down to us. There is extant, however, an epistle from Vittoria to her husband, entitled, "Epistola a Ferrante Francesco d'Avalos suo Consorte nella Rotta di Ràvenna," written in terza rima, containing thirty-seven stanzas. This composition, which cannot rank high from a poetical point of view, is a strange mixture of Christian religion and Pagan mythology. In it Vittoria calls on God to hear her vows on behalf of her father and husband, whom she likens to Hector and Achilles; and we then find her seeking consolation from the maritime deities who surround Ischia, and who reassure her as to the safety of her heroes' lives. With this epistle she sent him a device of a cupid encircled by a serpent, with the motto : " The love that virtue engenders may prudence preserve ;" (" Quell' amore che virtù produsse, prudenza conservi.") Owing to Trivulzio's influence, and perhaps by the still more efficacious means of a large ransom, Pescara was soon set at liberty, and lost no time in hastening to Naples, where Vittoria had removed from Ischia, so as to be within nearer reach of her husband.

The following description of Pescara, given by Giovio of him at this period of his life, speaks of him as being, " of a strong and sinewy frame, agile (destro), but not tall ; resolute and determined without any taint of indolence (fermissimo senza alcun pigro sugo), and a finished horseman, as well as foot-soldier. He had fine, large eyes, that were soft and mild in their expression, but when roused shot fire; his nose was·aquiline, his beard reddish. A man of few words, his answers were short, if not curt; while from his gestures and movements he was reputed proud and unbending. He was essentially Spanish, in his dress and habits alike, and," (characteristically of his nation) " Spanish was the only language he ever spoke, when in his daily intercourse with his wife, or in his dealings with Italians. He possessed the art of ingratiating himself with his soldiers, and his appointment shortly after to the command of the army was greeted with universal acclamation." Vittoria's joy on her husband's return is recorded in the following sonnet, written, however, many years after :—

[3] Laden with regal spoils and warlike prey
'Twas here my splendid sun came back to me ;

---

[3] Qui fece il mio bel sole a noi ritorno
Di regie spoglie carco e ricche prede :

Ah! with what grief those scenes again I see
In which his presence joyous made the day.
Laurels and palms lay strewn upon his way;
Save for the meed of fame no thought had he;
His bearing high, his converse wise and free,
Confirmed all good that men did of him say.

His glorious wounds, compliant to my prayers,
He showed to me, and told me when he met
And how he broke the ranks of hostile spears.
The joys that then he gave are changed to cares,
My thoughts run counter, and my eyes are wet
With a few sweet and many bitter tears.

It is said that Isabella, Duchess of Milan, ex-
claimed, on seeing him, "I would I too were a
man, Signor Marchese, if for nothing else but

---

Ahi! con quanto dolor l' occhio rivede
Quei lochi ov'ei mi fea già chiaro il giorno!
Di palme e lauro cinto era d' intorno,
D' onor, di gloria, sua sola mercede:
Ben potean far del grido sparso fede
L' ardito volto, il parlar saggio adorno.

Vinto da' prieghi miei poi ne mostrava
Le sue belle ferite, e 'l tempo e 'l modo
Delle vittorie sue tante e sì chiare.
Quanta pena or mi dà, gioia mi dava!
E in questo e in quel pensier piangendo godo
Tra poche dolci e assai lagrime amare.

to receive wounds in the face, as you have done, in order to see if they would become me as well as they do you."

On the 21st of February, 1513, Pope Julius II. died, and his successor on the Papal throne was Giovanni de' Medici, son of Lorenzo il Magnifico, and one of the youngest Pontiffs that ever sat in the chair of St. Peter, being only thirty-six years old. He took the name of Leo X., and his election, though unlooked for, met with general approbation. As his inclinations seemed to be of a more pacific nature than those of his predecessor, the French thought the moment a fitting one in which to regain their lost possessions in Italy, and prevailed on the Venetians to unite with them in invading Lombardy. The Marchese di Pescara, Fabrizio, and Prospero Colonna all hastened to the scene of action, and all assisted at the battle of Vicenza, which proved the most memorable event in this campaign. This battle was fought on the morning of the 7th of September, 1513, and in it the Venetians suffered a severe defeat, chiefly owing to the ignorance and rashness of Andrea Loredan, who urged his leader, Alviano, against his better judgment, to engage with the Spaniards.

Nothing of special importance occurred till the 1st of January, 1515, when Louis XII., King of France, died, and Francis I. of Angoulème, Duke of Valois, succeeded to the throne at the age of twenty-two. The war which Louis had waged unsuccessfully for fifteen years in Italy, Francis I. was but too eager to continue. In these wars we find Pescara ever to the fore, and now accompanied by his cousin Alfonso, Marchese del Vasto. Pescara, had at first resisted the entreaties of the youth to be with him, for he had appointed him heir to his name and estates, as after several years of married life he and Vittoria had no children, and the boy was, in every sense of the word, their adopted son ; but he yielded at last to the ardour of Alfonso and the pleadings of Vittoria, who urged in antique Roman language the cause of his kinsman. "Take the Marchese del Vasto with you," she said. "If he dies, there will be but one life the less ; and but one lineage the less should yours fail; all of which are not things so much to be feared and dreaded as that the dignity and glory of your ancestors should be in hands unworthy of such honours." She had herself prepared for the young warrior a magnificent tent, richly decorated with silk and embroidery, over the door of which she had worked a saying of Scipio Africanus · " He was never less idle, than when he was idle" ("Nuncquam minus otiosus, quam cum otiosus erat ille ").

Early in the following year, on the 15th of January, Ferdinand the Catholic expired. His grandson, Charles V., succeeded him as King of Spain, the Netherlands, Naples, and Sicily; and three years afterwards he added to these titles that of Emperor of Germany. One of the first acts of his reign was to sign with Francis I., on the 13th of August, 1516, the treaty of Noyon, which, for the time being, secured peace to all the western states of Europe, and which lasted till the death of Charles's other grandfather, the Emperor Maximilian, in 1519.

In this same year, 1516, Vittoria's eldest brother, Federigo, died. He had taken part with his father Fabrizio and Pescara in the war, and the Emperor Maximilian had just conferred on him the command of a troop of horse under his cousin Marcantonio, when he died.

It was also in this year that Vittoria was in Rome with her husband. It is to be regretted that no account of this has come down to us, for it was at this moment that the brilliancy of Leo X.'s court was at its height. It is probable that Vittoria here met some of the great men who afterwards became her intimate friends. Bembo and Sadoleto were now in Rome, and Giberti, who, young as he was, had already become the guide and adviser of Giulio de' Medici, offices which he still fulfilled when the Cardinal became Pope Clement VII.

In 1517 Leo X. bestowed a cardinal's hat on Prospero Colonna's nephew, Pompeo, and for the moment all smiled prosperously on Vittoria and her family.

Before passing on, however, to graver facts of Vittoria's history, the reader may be interested in an account given of her when she attended the wedding of Sigismund, King of Poland, and Bona Sforza, Duchessa di Bari, daughter of Gian Giacomo Sforza, Duke of Milan, and Isabella d' Aragona. The wedding took place at Naples with much pomp and state, and among the guests were Fabrizio Colonna, and the Marchese and Marchesa di Pescara. An eye-witness has described minutely the splendid appearance of Vittoria on this occasion: " Next came the most illustrious Marchesa di Pescara, mounted on a black and white steed, whose trappings were of crimson velvet with a fringe of gold and silver. Around her were six grooms, dressed in doublets and jerkins of blue and yellow satin. She herself had on a petticoat of brocade of dark red velvet, with large sprays of beaten gold on the petticoat. On her head she wore a coif of gold, with a cap of crimson satin, adorned with the same work of gold, and in her train were her six waiting-women, attired in blue damask."

During the war with France that occupied almost the whole of 1521, and the two succeeding years, one campaign followed another, and in all of them Pescara was ever to the fore, and ever gaining fresh honour. He wrested Milan from the French on the 19th of November, 1521, and from here he advanced upon and took Como. But the renown of this achievement must ever be obscured by disgrace to Pescara's name, for having pledged his word that the town should be spared, he was no sooner master of it than he gave it up to his soldiery, by whom it was mercilessly sacked.

The campaign of 1522 was a brilliant one for the Marchese. He relieved Pavia, then besieged by the French; he distinguished himself at the battle of Bicocca, took Lodi and Pizzighitone, and obliged Maréchal Lescun to capitulate at Cremona. He assisted largely in the taking of Genoa, where he allowed his soldiers to pillage and sack the town. As may well be imagined, such a succession of victories raised Pescara's reputation to the summit of fame,[4]

---

[4] Prescott speaks of him as "the ablest and most enterprising of the Imperial generals." (" Hist. of Charles V.")

and his name stands conspicuous among those of Charles's generals.

Towards the close of the next year, 1523, one of Charles's ablest generals was lost to him in the person of Prospero Colonna. He died at Milan, after several months' illness, and his end was hastened, it is supposed, by poison. Pescara and he had been brother officers in many a campaign, and during most of this year the Marchese had served successfully under his directions against the French, commanded by Bonnivet. Prospero's funeral took place at Milan with great solemnity, from where, eventually, his remains were removed to Naples.

In 1524 Pescara's fame was again in the ascendant, both at the Passage of the Sesia, and the siege of Alessandria. At the first of these two actions, Bonnivet being wounded and forced to retire, the command devolved on the Chevalier Bayard, who received his death-wound while covering the retreat of his defeated countrymen. Pescara did his utmost to preserve the life of his illustrious foe, and endeavoured to have him carried to a tent, in the hopes of tending his wounds. But all proved vain, and "Le Chevalier sans peur et sans reproche" breathed his last on the field of battle. Pescara caused his body to be embalmed, and sent with every exhibition of military respect and honour to his native country, the Dauphiné.[5] Bonnivet led the remains of his army back to France, only to return early in the following year, when Francis I. accompanied his forces. After several sharp fights around Milan, the King advanced to Pavia, where he was determined to conduct the siege in person, supported as he was by all the flower of the French nobility. The defence of the town had been entrusted to Antonio de Leyva, one of Charles's most prudent commanders, who neglected no opportunity for strengthening and protecting the city, or for procuring both food and ammunition for the hard-pressed garrison. On more than one occasion, Pescara and Del Vasto were able to bring in fresh supplies of provisions, and a large

---

[5] He was born at Grenoble, the capital of Dauphiné.

quantity of powder to replenish De Leyva's well-nigh exhausted stores, failing which Pavia would, without doubt, have been compelled to capitulate. In the meantime Francis had taken up his abode at the Certosa, but by far the larger share of his time and attention was given up to entertainments and revels, while he confided the weightier matters of war and the payment of his troops, to officers and ministers whose indifference to their master's concerns was only equalled by his own.

On the night of the 24th of February, 1526, the Imperialists, reduced to the last stage of despair, prepared for action, and on the morning of the next day, the far-famed battle of Pavia was fought. The Imperial forces outside the town were commanded by Pescara and the Viceroy Lannoy.[6] There is no need to enlarge on this well-known action here. Suffice it to say that the victory remained with the allies, and that Pescara's foresight and valour contributed in no small degree to this result. The

---

[6] He was a Fleming, and had been made Viceroy of Naples by Charles V.

French king had fought valiantly. Even when his horse had been killed under him, and he had received two slight wounds, he still made a heroic defence, till, further resistance being useless, he consented to surrender his sword to Lannoy, who treated him with all honour, and removed him for safety to the castle of Pavia. The Viceroy was anxious that he should be lodged in the castle at Milan, but the Duke was not keen that so responsible a charge should be entrusted to him. Francis therefore was taken to the stronghold of Pizzighitone, where twelve of his chosen companions were allowed to accompany him.

Pescara, who had fought with heroism, and whose life had more than once been saved by the devotion of his followers, was carried wounded to Milan, and it is with regret that we must turn from so brilliant a page of this gallant soldier's career to trace the downward course of his history, and his treacherous dealings with Morone, Vice-Chancellor of the Duchy of Milan. To explain the relationship between these two men, we must glance for a moment at the events occurring at that time in Milan.

The victory at Pavia had brought with it a fearful possibility to Italy in regard of the undue preponderance that would accrue to the Emperor's influence in the peninsula, and this dread had gathered weight when Charles endeavoured by every means in his power to gain possession of the Duchy of Milan. With this intent he urged the Duke to abdicate in his favour, offering him in return for the whole duchy, the castles of Milan and Cremona. Francesco Sforza, the last representative of an ill-fated race, was entirely under the sway of Girolamo Morone.[7]

---

[7] Guicciardini, who was no partisan of Morone, speaks of him as a man famous in his time for " intellect, eloquence, readiness, invention, and experience, and who had often bravely withstood the bitter trials and temptations of fortune." (Guicciardini, " Storia d'Italia," lib. xvi. cap. 3.)

Prescott, speaking òf Morone, says, "He was a man whose genius for intrigue and enterprise distinguished him in an age and country where violent factions, as well as frequent revolutions, affording great scope for such talents, produced or called them forth in great abundance." ("History of Charles V.")

Morone was endowed with great powers of mind, and a boundless ambition, together with a talent for intrigue, noted in an age—the age of Macchiavelli—when this quality was the mainspring of every action, and the very essence of all negotiation.   In spite of the hopeless look of affairs, Morone was by no means minded to sit passively by, and allow the grasping power of Charles to sweep the dukedom of Milan into his already too vast possessions, and he cast about for means to stem the coming torrent. He accordingly strove to form a league of an essentially Italian character, in which the Pope and the Venetians were to support Milan, and while this scheme would secure on the one hand safety and supremacy to the Sforza, it would also bring freedom and independence to Italy. The idea was a lofty and high-minded one, and though the means used to bring it about were not always of the purest, excuse may well be made for Morone, who was striving to save his patron and country, and whose end would undoubtedly be attained should the plot prove successful, while its failure would involve master and servant in one ruin. That he should have entered into communication with Pescara, and entrusted him with his secret, seems strange, for according to Guicciardini, he had often said, " There was no one in Italy of more malignity, or of less good faith than the Marchese." [8] On the other hand, Morone was aware how Pescara was smarting under the sense of unrequited services, and that his share in the victory of Pavia had not received the acknowledgments he considered due to him. The wily Chancellor dilated on all these fancied wrongs to the Marchese. He invited him to join in expelling the Spaniards from Italy, while he held out to him as the reward for his co-operation no less a bait than the throne of Naples. The post of Captain-General of the forces would also be his, and, should he lend himself in earnest to the plot and accept the overtures of Morone, the Pope was already prepared to grant him the investiture of the kingdom. Among the

---

[8] " Il Morone aveva detto più volte non essere uomo in Italia nè di malignità nè di minor fede di lui."—" Guic. Storia d'Italia," lib. xvi. cap 4.

intricacies of this labyrinth no clue seems satisfactory.[9] Some writers assert that the Marchese entered eagerly into the conspiracy, being exasperated by the want of appreciation shown him by Charles. Others again maintain that he acted throughout as a loyal servant of the Emperor, who, by listening to every suggestion made to him, was better able to unravel the scheme, and acquaint his master with the danger against which he would have to provide. Be this as it may, all appeared for the moment to be advancing; the Venetian Government promised their aid ; the Pope had despatched a special messenger, one Domenico Sauli, to assure to Pescara the crown of his promised kingdom, when the latter, in order, it is said, to gain time, raised such difficulties and questions that all was brought suddenly to a standstill. From the statements of Guicciardini and Ripamonte, as well as from the written confession of Morone himself, it appears that the Marchese had in writing disclosed to

---

[9] " Qui l'istoria si aggira tra inestricabili incertezze."— Capponi, " Storia della Republica di Firenze," lib. vi. cap. 6.

Charles the whole design, who in return bade
him still negotiate with the Chancellor, and
unravel more of the plot. In order to do so,
Pescara invited Morone to meet him at Novara,
under colour of inquiring further into the details
of the affair. Previous to their interview he
had prevailed on Antonio de Leyva to assist
him, and for this purpose De Leyva was con-
cealed behind a piece of tapestry in the room,
from whence he could overhear every word
that fell from the Chancellor's lips. Morone,
wholly unsuspicious of the deed of perfidy that
was being practised upon him, omitted no
detail of his entire scheme; and when the
listeners had gleaned every particular, they
caused him to be arrested in the name of the
Emperor, taken to Pavia, and confined in the
castle there. While in prison, Pescara and
De Leyva visited him, and, under torture, drew
from him a full confession of what he had
already narrated at Novara, which they also
compelled him to set down in writing. This
document, which has but lately come to light,
bears testimony to the ingenuity of Morone,

while it shows up the treachery of Pescara, who had passed his word to the Chancellor never to betray him. The epithet of traitor must therefore attach itself to Pescara, for allowing that he listened to the scheme only in the capacity of a faithful vassal of the Emperor, how can his treachery to Morone, and his promise not to betray him, be explained away? The judgment passed by Ripamonte on the Marchese, and which later records seem to confirm, declares: "There was not to be found in his day any one more deeply dyed in perfidy, or more courageous in arms." [1]

In the meantime Pescara had received a letter from Vittoria, in which she entreats him "not to be dazzled by the snare of a kingdom, nor allow his loyalty and faith to his master to be sullied in such a way; that for herself she was not ambitious of being the wife of a king, but rather of that great general, whose valour and courtesy in peace or in war prevailed alike over monarchs." This letter is quoted only

---

[1] "Non esservi stato ai suoi dì alcuno più infame in perfidia, nè più valoroso nelle armi."—Ripamonte, Hist. Pat.

by Giovio; but there can be no doubt that
Vittoria had heard of the temptation assailing
her husband, and that she exerted her influence
to the utmost to recall him to a sense of honour
and duty. It is said that on hearing of the
Marchese's treachery, she exclaimed, " There
exists no greater enemy to man than overmuch
prosperity."

But the agitation which all this complicated
business had brought with it, proved too
much for Pescara. His frame, enfeebled by
the privations through which he had passed,
and by the wounds received at Pavia and else-
where, sank under the load of anxiety and
excitement. He fell desperately ill, or as
Visconti puts it, " cadde in istrano malore," as
though it were some uncommon malady; and
feeling his hours were numbered, he sent in all
haste for his cousin, the Marchese del Vasto.
To him he commended his wife; and confirm-
ing to him the heritage of all his estates, he
breathed his last on the 25th of November,
1525, in the thirty-third year of his age.

Rumour hinted that his death was hastened

by poison, administered by order of the Emperor, to avenge the share the Marchese had taken in Morone's conspiracy,[2] but all evidence is wanting to confirm so improbable a story.

Vittoria, on hearing how serious a form her husband's illness had assumed, had at once started from Naples for Milan. The last time she had seen him was for three short days in October, 1522, when her mother, having died while returning from a pilgrimage to Loreto, Pescara had hastened to Naples to comfort his wife. It was, therefore, three years since they had met, and little had they thought that was to be their last meeting on earth. Vittoria had hurried through Rome, and had gone as far as Viterbo, when the fatal news reached her. On receiving it the shock was great, and for a long time she remained in a state of unconsciousness, and though Bembo's declaration

---

[2] Morone survived him only four years; he died suddenly in 1529, at a moment when he was in favour with Pope Clement VII.—Capponi, " Storia della Republica di Firenze," lib. vi. cap. 9.

that she contemplated committing suicide is doubtful, there can be no question that her grief at first was ungovernable, and that some time elapsed before she regained her serenity of mind. On the 30th of November Pescara's funeral took place at Milan with great state, and soon afterwards his remains were removed to Naples, and buried with those of his family in the curious, grand old church of San Domenico Maggiore.

Vittoria was not present at the funeral ceremonies: she returned to Rome, and having obtained leave from Pope Clement VII., she retired to the convent of S. Silvestro in Capite, which was under the special patronage of the Colonna family, and here passed the early days of her widowhood. Her first impulse was to take the veil, and in a life of seclusion devote herself to prayer and mourning. The Pope, however, refused to sanction such a step, and her friends and relations prevailing on her to relinquish her purpose, she remained only a few months at S. Silvestro.

The absence of any allusion to her husband's treachery throughout the whole of Vittoria's writings may at first awaken our surprise. When we reflect, however, how time soothes for us its "whips and scorns;" and how, from the smallest troubles of life down to the great reality of Death, who, in taking from us our loved ones, leaves only the memory of how good, how dear they were, we cease to wonder. We acknowledge that she was right in dwelling only on the higher, better qualities of her husband, and we are grateful that Time and the grave in mercy glossed over for her the stain which history must ever attach to Pescara's name.[3]

Heath Wilson,[4] speaking of her, says :—

" Vittoria wept for him (Pescara) ; none could judge better than she, with her clear, moral perceptions, of his errors, but her affection for him never failed, and after his death she remembered only his brilliant qualities and their mutual happiness."

Her retreat at San Silvestro was disturbed

---

[3] " Death consecrated her husband for Vittoria, as death canonized Laura for Petrarch."—J. A. Symonds, " Italian Literature."

[4] "Life of Michelangelo," by Heath Wilson, chap. xvi.

by "wars and tumults of wars," in which her own family bore a conspicuous part.

The treaty concluded between Charles V. and Francis I., by which the French monarch had regained his liberty, was totally disregarded by him when he was once more in his own territories, and in his own words, "once more a king." Charles, unable to obtain by negotiation the fulfilment of his promises, resorted to war, and Italy was again the scene of disturbance and bloodshed. The Pope, having absolved Francis from all the oaths and engagements to which he had pledged himself while a prisoner at Madrid, the Emperor's wrath was roused against Clement; and the Colonna, from their position as head of the Ghibelline party in Rome, and partisans of Charles, warmly espoused his cause.

Before affairs had become so serious, Vittoria's brother, Ascanio Colonna, had advised her leaving Rome, and, following his counsel, she retired in September of this year to Marino. From here, alarmed at the warlike aspect of things, she wrote to Gianmatteo Giberti, who was chancellor to the Pope, and possessed of immense influence over him, to entreat him to do his utmost to reconcile the contending parties, and to bring about peace. But Clement, smarting under the recollection of former wrongs, was not disposed to listen to any overtures; he deprived Pompeo Colonna of his cardinalate, and Ascanio and others of their lands, at the same time freeing their vassals from their allegiance. Vittoria, on hearing how fruitless her efforts had proved, left Marino, going first to Naples, and from there to Ischia. The following sonnet, in which "she finds comfort in spiritual meditations under the adversities which befall the Colonna," may have been written at this time :—

[5] Though earthly tyrants with resistless brand,
Within, without my column smite alway,
In flames by night, in clouds of smoke by day,
I see that other heaven-sent pillar stand

---

[5] Se l' imperio terren con mano armata
  Batte la mia Colonna entro e d'intorno,
  La notte in foco e in chiara nube il giorno
  Veggio quella celeste alta e beata,

Of God's high grace, which I may not withstand ;
For so entranced am I, should I essay
From earthly love to turn, it still would stay
Within my heart, and hold me with firm hand.

Methinks that then a spell of peaceful rest
Is shown to me, the which I love to see.
I know not if my soul with fancies blest,
Deceives itself for its own good, while He
My generous Lord, without shows dark and drear,
But flows within with greater radiance clear.

The year 1527 was now dawning on Italy ; a
year that, to quote Muratori, was the most fatal
and disastrous that had ever been in Italy (" un
anno de' più funesti e lagrimevoli che s'abbia mai
avuto in Italia "), and which was to acquire so
sinister a renown from the sack of Rome ; that

---

Sua mercè, con la mente : onde portata
    Sono in parte talor, che se in me torno
    Dal nàtural amor, che fa soggiorno
    Dentr' al mio cor, ben spesso richiamata,

Mi par per lungo spazio e queto e puro
    Quanto discerno, e quanto sento caro.
    Non so se l' alma per suo ben vaneggia,
O pur se'l largo mio signor, che avaro
    Di fuor si mostra al tempo freddo oscuro,
    Dentro più dell' usato arde e lampeggia.

deed of shame and horror to all Christendom, which must reflect everlasting ignominy on the reign of Charles V. His troops, under the command of the Constable of Bourbon,[6] to whom Charles had promised the investiture of the Duchy of Milan, were backed by large companies of German mercenaries, who, glowing with all the fervour of converts to Luther's new doctrines, clamoured to be led to Rome, and prove the ardour of their faith by sweeping the Eternal City, and all that it contained, from the face of the earth. Early in May the Imperialists laid siege to Rome, but their leader, Bourbon, while planting a ladder against the walls, received his death-wound, and his soldiers, infuriated by the loss of their general, and determined to avenge him, stormed the town, and, carrying all before them, put the garrison to the sword. Cries of "Liberty, Colonna, Empire," resounded from every quarter; and the Colonna, bent on avenging private grievances,

---

[6] Charles, Duke of Montpensier, Constable of Bourbon, had offended his sovereign, Francis I., and taken service under the Emperor.

sacked the Vatican, and pillaged the suburbs, with all that they could lay hands on belonging to their hated rivals, the Orsini. For seven months Rome was in the hands of the victors, and never, under Goth or Vandal, had such lawlessness and outrages been committed as were now perpetrated by "Catholic Spaniards and Lutheran Germans." Vittoria's anguish over these horrors, in which her family were so closely involved, was extreme. She wrote bitterly to Pompeo Colonna, and beseechingly to the Marchese del Vasto, imploring them both to use their utmost endeavours to put an end to iniquities " which, had her parents or her husband been alive, would never have been permitted or countenanced by those of her name and family." Her father Fabrizio, had died at Aversa in March, 1520, full of years and honours. Macchiavelli had so high an opinion of his military talents that he introduces him into his " Arte della Guerra." Ariosto speaks of him as, " La gran Colonna del nome romano." [7]

---

[7] " Orlando Furioso," Canto xiv.

Vittoria's own words written, as the reader will see many years after this date, explain why she could not celebrate his memory, her pen being devoted to lamentations for her dead husband.

8 The antique virtues of my Roman sire,
   If I should seek in numbers to express,
   An inward love, a filial tenderness
   Would stay my hand, and check the fond desire.
   Nor were it meet this low and humble lyre,
   Attuned to one chaste love, one sore distress,
   That wastes my hours and days in vain excess
   Of grief, to sound his glories should aspire.

'Tis not lest light I take from my high sun
My voice is silent.  Love's capricious might
By reason uncontroll'd the will compels.

---

8 S'io non descrivo in carte il più che umano
   Del roman nostro padre alto valore,
   Interna carità, pietoso amore
   Fa mancare il pensier, cader la mano.
Nè può le glorie sue l' umile e piano
   Stile agguagliar, che sol d' un casto ardore
   Ragionar sa, che tutti i giorni e l' ore
   Fa ch 'io consumi lagrimando in vano.

Non perch' io toglia lume al sole altero
   Di scriver resto, ch' amorosa forza
   Spinge il voler che la ragion non curá.

Both loves to me are sacred ; but the one
Bids me refrain, the other bids me write,
Alike with both lamenting memory dwells.

To return to Vittoria.   Her fortune and sub-
stance were devoted in the midst of these dis-
asters in helping all who suffered in this terrible
siege, and in ransoming prisoners ; so that to use
Visconti's words, " She seemed like a star of
peace in the midst of this perturbed sky."
These acts of mercy met with their reward in
a short space of time; for in the following
year, Ascanio and Camillo Colonna, and the
Marchese del Vasto having been made prisoners
at the naval fight of Salerno, when Andrea
Doria and his nephew Filippino defeated the
allied French and Spanish navies, Vittoria en-
treated Filippino to set her kinsmen free, with
which request he immediately complied, in
appreciation for all she had done the previous
year for his suffering countrymen.

---

Ben servo l' uno e l' altro amore intero,
Ma l' un tacer, l' altro parlar mi sforza ;
E d'ambedue sospiro in veste oscura.

# II.

THE first part of Vittoria's life may now be looked upon as closed, and in the second phase now opening out, she comes before us in her better-known character of poetess and writer. She gives us in her first sonnet the reason of her writings, and how she has taken to this as a resource for the outpouring of her griefs :—

[9] I write to ease that inner grief alone,
Which feeds my heart, desiring other none,
Not to add lustre to my glorious sun,
Whose spoils bequeathed to earth are honour s own
Just cause have I to weep and make my moan ;
And if for him is lesser glory won,
With other pen, in wiser words be done
His tale, and snatch'd from death his name be known.

---

[9] Scrivo sol per sfogar l' interna doglia
   Di che si pasce il cor, ch' altro non vole,
   E non per giunger lume al mio bel sole,
   Che lasciò in terra sì onorata spoglia.
Giusta cagione a lamentar m' invoglia ;
   Ch' io scemi la sua gloria assai mi dole ;
   Per altra penna e più saggie parole
   Verrà chi a morte il suo gran nome toglia.

Pure faith, deep passion, and intensest pain
May plead for me, when they so strong are seen,
That neither time nor reason give relief.
It is a bitter plaint, and no sweet strain
With blinding sighs, and not a voice serene,
Wins me no praise for style, but praise for grief.

R. S. P.

During the first seven years of her widow-hood her time and talents are devoted, to the exclusion of other subjects, in lamentations over "il mio bel sole," as she invariably calls her husband, and in " erecting a monument to Pescara's memory by her poems, so honour-able to his name, that (as long as the world lasts) it will in consequence ever be famous and illustrious among us." [1] Her brothers

---

La pura fè, l' ardor, l' intensa pena
   Mi scusi appo ciascun, grave cotanto
   Che nè ragion nè tempo mai l' affrena.
Amaro lagrimar, non dolce canto,
   Foschi sospiri e non voce serena,
   Di stil no, ma di duol mi danno il vanto.

[1] " Colle sue rare e maravigliose Rime, ella fece un sepolcro così onorevole al nome di suo marito, che finchè il mondo duri, sara preciò sempre celebrato ed illustrato fra noi."—Fr. Agostino della Chiesa.

were anxious she should marry again, and her hand was on several occasions sought in marriage by some of the noblest in the land, but her reply in these circumstances was ever the same: "That although her beautiful sun had disappeared to all, he still shone for her, and that alike in brightness or obscurity she would guard intact the faith of her heart."

Visconti assumes that it was now she composed the sonnet given below, and which he imagines addressed to the Duchessa di Francavilla. In it she likens herself to a juniper-tree, ·and repels all suitors in the same way the tree repels the assaults of wind and tempest :—

[2] That juniper which self-secure doth grow,
Though angry tempests try her power to wrest ;
And neither fearful covers up her breast,
Nor sheds her foliage on the earth below:

---

[2] Qual bel ginebro, cui d' intorno cinge
Irato vento, che nè le sue foglie
Sparge, nè i suoi rami apre, anzi raccoglie
La cima, e tutto 'n sè stesso si stringe

E

So doth my soul, O lady, steadfast glow,
Though by assailing Fortune oft opprest;
But on high cares and noble aims doth rest,
Repulsing calmly every daring foe.

And thus my soul, protected by the thought
Of that belovèd sun whom I adore,
Victorious will arise from every strife.
The tree by Nature has been likewise taught
Its foes to quell : so Reason wills e'en more
That from my griefs my faith should spring to life.

The greater part of the year 1533 she
passed at Ischia, and the following sonnet, in
which she gives her reasons for living there,
was probably written at this time :—

Qual sia l' animo mio, donna, depinge
  Che fortuna combatte e non si scioglie
  Dall' alte cure ed onorate voglie,
  E chi vincerlo pensa addietro spinge.

Perchè sicuro, sotto i gran pensieri
  Ristretto di quel sol ch' ama ed adora,
  Vincitor d' ogni guerra altero riede.
A quell' arbor natura insegna i fieri
  Nemici contrastar; ed in me ancora
  Ragion vuol che nel mal cresca la fede.

³ On this rough rock I dwell, this lonely shore;
Like the lorn bird that shuns both verdant grove
And limpid stream, from all on earth I love
And from myself to hide me evermore.
For towards that sun I worship and adore,
Forth flies my soul, and though its pinions move
In devious course or slow, when I reprove
From other flights recalled to this 'twill soar.

And when elate and glad it cleaves its way
Whither I send it, the brief joy transcends
The raptures of all earthly happiness.
But could it only worthily portray
That radiant form, where mind with beauty blends,
Then had I foretaste here of future bliss.

---

³ Vivo su questo scoglio orrido e solo,
    Quasi dolente augel che 'l verde ramo
    E l' acqua pura abborre; e a quelli ch' amo
    Nel mondo ed a me stessa ancor m' involo,
Perchè espedito al sol che adoro e colo,
    Vada il pensiero.   E sebben quanto bramo
    L' ali non spiega, pur quando io 'l richiamo
    Volge dall' altre strade a questa il volo.

E'n quel punto che giunge lieto e ardente
    Là 've l' invio, sì breve gioia avanza
    Qui di gran lunga ogni mondan diletto.
Ma se potesse l' alta sua sembianza
    Formar, quant' ella vuol l' accesa mente,
    Parte avrei forse qui del ben perfetto.

Somewhat later in life we find her writings more devoted to religious subjects, while her advice and sympathy on such matters were sought by high and low, who turned to her for guidance and help in their doubts and perplexities. The following sonnet addressed to her by Margaret of Valois, Queen of Navarre,[4] shows in what high veneration Vittoria was held :—

[5] Oh! happy thou, whose ardent spirit flies
Unto our Lord to whom thy heart is bent,
And kindlest all with thee to wait intent
On Him, who keeps us always in His eyes.
Ah! hapless me, whom much He doth despise
That with weak step and slow to Him I went :
False words, vain thoughts, ill deeds I now lament
And plead for pardon in repentant sighs.

---

[4] She was sister of Francis I., and first wife of Henri d'Albret, consequently grandmother of King Henry IV. of France.

[5] Felice voi, che con gli spirti ardenti
    Avete il cor al mio Signor rivolto,
    E accendete ognun a star raccolto
    In Lui, che verso noi tien gli occhi intenti.
Misera me, ch' ai passi infermi e lenti
    Seguito ho Lui, che me sprezzato ha molto :
    Ond' or del van desio, fallace e stolto
    L' alma si pente e trae sospir cocenti.

But thou, who mid the heavenly host dost shine,
Beseech the King of Heaven that with His hand
He raise me up and fold me in His breast.
And as thou hast attained to light divine,
So act that others may beside thee stand,
And enter with thee into perfect rest.

The following quotation from Rota's " Life of Vittoria Colonna," will serve also to prove how her mind, " set on things above," was able to help and direct others in their troubles :— " It was already the seventh year since the Marchese de Pescara had ascended to a better life, when Vittoria, having vainly made trial by every effort to free her soul from sadness and sorrow, recognized but too clearly the misery of those who live according to the appetites of nature ; and that the goods of this earth re- semble the rose, for both in their birth and their growth the thorns are inseparably joined

---

Prega, e voi, che degli eletti sete
    Per me de' Cieli il Rè, che la sua mano
    Mi tenga sopra, e mi raccolga in seno.
E poi che scorto il vero lume avete,
    Fate, che ancor non sia per gli altri vano,
    Ma, ch' il provi ciascun chiaro e sereno.

to them, therefore she disposed herself to the raising of her mind above earthly affairs, and fixed them on divine ones, convinced that this was the only means of freeing the soul from those affections whence come most of this world's bitternesses. In fact, she adopted a spiritual life, and thus fixed her soul on heavenly things, and so entirely forgetting earthly love, she became engrossed with heavenly, and from this time forward devoted her pen to sacred writings, refraining almost entirely from secular rhymes, which had been hitherto the general subject of her compositions."

She did not exclude altogether the interests of this world from her daily life, for in 1536 she was in Rome with her adopted son, the Marchese del Vasto, her brother Ascanio, and his wife Giovanna d'Aragona,[6] visiting the wonders of the eternal city. While contemplating some of the splendours of the past, Vittoria remarked with a deep sigh, " Ah! how blessed

---

[6] She was daughter of Ferdinand, Duca di Montalto, and her sister, Maria, was the wife of the Marchese del Vasto.

were they who lived in such glorious times."
Molza,[7] who was present, rejoined, " Their hap-
piness would have been greater could they
have known you."

This same year she went to Ischia, but only
for a short time, returning soon to Rome,
where Paul III. (Farnese) held a brilliant
reception in her honour. ·During the time she
was in Rome Charles V. was also there, though
for the short period of four days only. Rossa
tells us that " the Emperor condescended to
visit in their houses, Donna Giovanna d'Ara-
gona, Duchessa di Tagliacozzo, wife of Ascanio
Colonna, and Vittoria Colonna, Marchesa di
Pescara."[8] To this sister-in-law Vittoria ad-
dressed two sonnets, one of which we give
here :—

[9] Could I my neck from out the yoke but free,
  O, lady mine, and turn awhile my sight,

---

[7] Molza was one of the most learned scholars of his day,
and was Vittoria's instructor in the art of poetry.
[8] " History of the Things of Naples under Charles V."
[9] S' io potessi sottrar dal giogo alquanto,
    Madonna, il collo e volger i pensieri

Whole and detached from that my other light,
Changing to smiles my tears I'd sing of thee.
Most sweet the style, most soft the song should be
To honour thee, and praise thy merits tried ;
For neither crowns nor regal robes decide
The virtues high that form true sovereignty.

While Heaven to thee was lavish, my star shone
With niggard beams, 'twas right my sun should
    rise
And hold my gaze intent on him alone,
Hiding my vision from thy paradise,
Lest should thy praises lustreless appear
Or turn me from my wonted sorrows dear.

Early in 1537 she went to Lucca, and from
there to Ferrara, where Duke Ercole II., of

---

    Dalla mia luce altrove sciolti e' ntieri,
      Li porrei in voi, volgendo in riso il pianto.
Farei dolce lo stil, soave il canto,
      Per dir de' vostri onori e pregi altieri ;
  ' Chè l' alte sue virtù son regni veri,
      Non corona, nè scettro, o regal manto.

  Ma a voi fu 'l ciel sì largo, e a me la stella
    Sì parca, che s'oppon bene il mio sole
    Fra 'l vostro paradiso e gli occhi miei,
Che ritlen con la vista, e come suole
    La ferma in lui, per non veder men bella
    La vostra lode, e tôrmi i cari omei !

Este, was reigning, who received her with every mark of honour  Vittoria's chief reason for staying at Ferrara was to comply with Ochino's[1] wish that she should persuade the Duke to allow the Capuchins to establish their order in the city. This request was granted without delay, and a piece of land on the banks of the Po was presented by the Duke to Ochino, who came in the autumn of this year to Ferrara to install the brotherhood in their new possession.

Vittoria was received as a guest worthy of all attention, and Duke Ercole spared no pains in attracting all the great and learned in Lombardy and Venice to his court to meet her. One of the brightest ornaments of this court, Ludovico Ariosto, who had already sung Vittoria's praises,[2] had died four years previous to this date.

The inhabitants of Verona were anxious Vittoria should visit their city, and the Bishop,

---

[1] Fra Bernardino of Siena, better known as Ochino, was a Capuchin monk, learned, highly esteemed, and so eloquent and earnest in his preaching, that it was hyperbolically said, he could melt the very stones to tears.

[2] See page 109, &c.

Monsignore Giberti, in the hopes of persuading her to do so, sent his secretary, Francesco della Torre, to invite her to the episcopal palace. The fruitlessness of the mission is related in a letter to Cardinal Bembo, in which the emissary declares in high-flown language that he would either have been outlawed by the Duke, or stoned by the people, so great was the universal indignation that Ferrara should be deprived of its chief ornament to enrich Verona.

It was about this time that in spite of failing health, Vittoria was eager to make a pilgrimage to the Holy Land. Some of her sonnets dwell entirely on Palestine, and we give one in which her hopes for its conquest revive.

[3] I feel the flowering hope within me rise,
Which I had wither'd thought, and dead to be,
That Holy, but neglected Land to see
Which the great Tomb adorns and glorifies.

---

[3] Già si rinverde la gioiosa speme,
Che quasi secca era da me sbandita,
Di veder l' alma e mal da noi gradita
Terra che 'l gran sepolcro adorna e preme.

I hear that gallant men alike despise
Hardships and death, while in them strong and free
Burns jealously that faith which lost have we,
Their blood to others quickening seed supplies

So fruitful, that though few are the elect
They shall with voices loud great numbers gain,
To call upon their true, though unknown Lord.
So to our shame, with life-giving effect
The sign of the all-glorious Cross again
Shall be proclaimed, and through the world adored.

She was prevailed on to relinquish her purpose of visiting the Holy Land at the instance of the Marchese del Vasto, who pointed out to her the perils of such a journey, and urged on her the advisability of settling in Rome. To this she consented, and towards the end of the year we find her established there in the zenith

---

Odo ch' or gente intrepida non teme
    Tormenti e morte, anzi è cotanto ardita
    Alla fede fra noi quasi smarrita,
    Che 'l sangue loro agli altri è vivo seme
Sì fecondo, che sol ben pochi eletti
    Fan da molti chiamar ad alta voce
    Il verace signor già loro ignoto ;
Ed a scorno di noi, con vivi effetti
    Il segno ancor dell' onorata croce
    Faran con maggior gloria al mondo noto.

of her fame, sought out and surrounded by all
who for learning and talent were of note in the
Eternal City.  "There was no man of great
name in the world of letters," says Symonds,
"who did not set his pride on being thought
her friend.  The collections of letters and poems
belonging to that period abound in allusions to
her genius, her holiness, and her great beauty." [4]
Among these can be named Giovio, who dedi-
cated to her his work in seven volumes of the
"Life of Pescara;" Ludovico Martelli, who
addressed some of his sonnets to her; Veronica
Gambara, who like herself was a poetess and
writer of no mean order, and who also passed
the greater part of her life in "faithful widow-
hood."  Castiglione was also among those who
came under the elevating influence that Vittoria
shed around her, and his well-known work,
"The Courtier" (Il Cortigiano) was written as
much to please her as his royal patron, Louis
XII. of France.[5]

---

[4] "Italian Literature."  J. A. Symonds.

[5] Baldassare Castiglione was born in 1476, at Cesatico,
in the province of Mantua.  He was some time at the

It is evident that Vittoria's house was the centre both of literary and religious discussion, for Cardinals Pole and Contarini, the heads of Ochino's party, were her intimate friends. Ochino himself was well known to her, and his advanced views, in which however she did not concur, were of great interest to her. On account of her close friendship with him, the Inquisition kept a suspicious watch over all Vittoria's deeds, sayings, and writings; and we can judge how strict that scrutiny was, when we know that twenty years after her death a noble Florentine was condemned to the stake by the Inquisition in Rome, one of the principal charges against him being that he had belonged to the circle of Giulia Gonzaga, and Vittoria Colonna.[6] How far Vittoria was from

---

court of Urbino in the capacity of court poet. He went to Spain as Nuncio, and ended his days at Toledo in 1529. His work was translated by Thomas Hoby into English in 1561.

[6] This was Pietro Carnesecchi, a man of rank and learning, who had adopted some of the tenets of Luther. Pius V. in 1566 demanded his person from the Grand Duke Cosimo I., who gave him up to the officers of ome,

agreeing with Ochino's views may be gathered from the following extract from a letter she wrote to Marcello Corbino, afterwards Pope Marcello II., in which, speaking of Ochino, who had embraced the new doctrines, she says:—

"I grieve deeply that the more he thinks to excuse himself, the more he accuses himself; and the more he thinks to save others from shipwreck, the more he exposes them to the deluge; he being himself outside the ark which saves and gives security." These thoughts may have been in her mind when she composed this sonnet:—

[7] Him shall no worldly fears, no war dismay
    Whose peace is made with Heaven. No winter's cold
    Shall chill his breast who therein doth enfold
    The sacred fervour of celestial day.

---

and at the same time wrote earnestly to the Pope to save nim. This Pius seems to have been inclined to do, on condition Carnesecchi would renounce his tenets. On his refusal, he was handed over to the Inquisition, publicly beheaded, and his body afterwards burned.

[7] Non dee temer del mondo affanni o guerra
    Colui ch' ave col ciel tranquilla pace:
    Che nuoce il gielo a quel ch' entro la face
    Del calor vero si rinchiude e serra?

The fetters of the world are weak to stay
The soul whose flight is vigorous and bold ;
No insults shame him who doth silence hold,
And prayeth most for them who farthest stray.

The tower that on the living Rock is set,
(Whereby alone is safety unto men),
Assault from near or far alike defies ;
In vain the fowler spreads his crafty net,
'Mid the dank vapours of the stagnant fen,
To snare the eagle soaring through the skies.

Another of her nearer friends was Cardinal
Pietro Bembo, who shone as a leader in the
movement then on foot, to restore Italian in
place of Latin, as the language of Italy. He
was a Venetian, and for more than fifty years
was looked upon as the guide and director in

---

Non preme il grave peso della terra
   Lo spirito che vola alto e vivace ;
   Nè fan biasmo l' ingiurie all' uom che tace,
   E prega più per chi più pecca ed erra.

Non giova saettar presso o lontano
   Torre fondata in quella viva pietra,
   Ch' ogni edificio uman rende sicuro ;
Nè tender reti con accorta mano
   Fra l' aer basso paludoso e scuro
   Contra l' augel che sopra 'l ciel penetra.

all questions relating to literature. More than one of Vittoria's sonnets were addressed to him, and were answered by him in the same style. Muratori speaks in high praise of one of these sonnets of Vittoria's, which is given below, and says, " This sonnet would suffice to convince us (were we not already certain of it) of the happy wit (felice ingegno) of the Marchesa di Pescara."

[8] To Pietro Bembo.

If my fair sun before he ceased to shine
On this fair earth, had touch'd thee with his rays,
Thy soul had kindled to so warm a blaze
That endless fame were his and praise were thine.

For were his name link'd to that style divine,
Which puts antiquity to shame, and stays
The shaft of envy, guarded thus always,
No second death his spirit could confine.

---

[8] Se v' accendeva il mio bel sole amato,
　　Con l' ardente virtù dei raggi suoi,
　　Pria che tornasse al ciel mill' anni e poi
　　Ei più chiaro saria, voi più lodato.
Il nome suo col vostro stil pregiato,
　　Ond' han gli antichi scorno, invidia noi,
　　A mal grado del tempo avreste voi
　　Dal secondo morir sempre guardato.

Could I instil my passion in thy breast,
Or could I borrow all thy wit from thee,
Fit pinions then were ours for loftiest flight :
But now perchance Heaven's wrath on thee may rest
Who other theme hast chosen ; and on me
That I should dare to speak of such a light.

Another of her friends was Giovanni Guidic-cioni. He was born at Lucca in 1500, and died in 1541. Paul III. made him Bishop of Fossombrone, and he was celebrated in his day for his songs and sonnets, most of which relate to the woes and miseries of Italy.

A list might be given enumerating the names of those who laid claim to literary celebrity, and who aspired to Vittoria's friendship ; but pre-eminent among them all stands out that of Michelangelo Buonarroti, sufficient in itself to cast an eternal halo around her whom he loved so nobly. No precise date can be given for

---

Deh, potess' io mandar nel vostro petto
    L'ardor ch' io sento, e voi nel mio ingegno !
    Chè avrei forse al gran vol conformi l' ale !
Chè cosi temo 'l ciel non prenda a sdegno
    Voi, perchè preso avete altro soggetto,
    Me, ch' ardisco parlar d'un lume tale.

F

the commencement of their friendship, but 'it must have been some little time after 1534, the year in which Michelangelo came to Rome. Grimm[9] places their first meeting in 1536, but all other historians fix the date at 1538, when Michelangelo was sixty years old, alone and solitary, without a ray of hope as to the happiness still in store for him. The sadness and gloom that hung over Michelangelo's life arose from different causes. Though imbued with strong family affections, his temper had been tried by quarrels with his brothers. He had also been irritated by the way in which they had endeavoured to extort money from him, and to induce their father to profit by his talents. His natural bent inclined him to solitude. He mixed rarely in the society of his fellow-beings, and his own written words, " I have no friends: I need none, and wish for none," have in them almost a boastful desire for isolation. A few years previously his old father Ludovico, and his brother Buonarroto had died.

---

[9] " Leben Michelangelos." Hermann Grimm. Hanover, 1873.

Apart from these sorrows he was in perplexity as to his work. Regardless of an engagement to the Duke of Urbino, the Pope (Paul III.) insisted that Michelangelo should carry out the design for the decoration of the Sixtine Chapel. In vain he pleaded his contract with the Duke, Paul would not be gainsaid, and his impetuosity and determination swept away all opposition.

It was in the midst of these troubles and anxieties that Michelangelo's friendship with Vittoria was formed, "which," says Heath Wilson, "was marked by the depth and grandeur of his character in its devotion and vitality, and returned by her with an admiration of his gifts and talents which was unbounded."[1] The relationship between the two is a pleasant one to dwell on. To the old man it was a friendship fitted in every way to cheer and lighten the gloom in which he lived and worked. From his poems we see that he loved women. But from none of his sonnets do we glean that happiness came to him from such love; whereas

---

[1] "Life and Works of Michelangelo Buonarotti," by Charles Heath Wilson. London, 1876.

sorrow and resignation over unrequited passion are expressed in most of his writings.

To Vittoria the friendship with Michelangelo was a source of unmixed joy. Her admiration of his genius and talents was great, and the knowledge of her softening influence upon him must have brought with it a peculiar charm. How strong this influence was we know from his own words, for he says that "from the rough model wherein he was born, she had reformed and remade him" (nato rozzo modello di sè, era poi stato da lei riformato e rifatto). Condivi,[2] speaking of the friendship between them, says:—"He particularly loved the Marchesana di Pescara, of whose divine understanding (divino spirito) he was enamoured, and he was in return dearly loved by her. He received from her many letters full of honest and true love, as is wont to proceed from such natures. He likewise addressed to her numerous sonnets full of wit and sweet desire. She removed several times from Viterbo to other

---

[2] "Vita di Michelangelo Buonarotti; scritta da Ascanio Condivi."

places, whither she had gone for relaxation and
to pass the summer, and came to Rome for no
other purpose but to see Michelangelo ; and he
bore her such true affection that I remember to
have heard him say that his only regret when
he went to take his last look at her after death,
was, that he had only kissed her hand, and not
her face and forehead as well. Her death
caused him to be distracted with grief, and to
remain as one insensible." That he painted
more than one picture for Vittoria seems certain,
though we have no indication as to which these
are.[3] On the completion of one of them, she
writes to him :—" Your works forcibly awaken
the judgment of all who look at them, and I

---

[3] Speaking of the Crucifixion, with the Virgin and St.
John, Sir J. C. Robinson, in his " Drawings of Michel-
angelo and Raffello in the University of Oxford " (1870),
says :—" The famous composition, one phase or preliminary
stage of which is represented by this drawing, is known to
have been undertaken by Michelangelo for his friend, the
celebrated Vittoria Colonna, Marchioness of Pescara. It
does not seem very certain what shape the work was in-
tended finally to assume, but it is probable that Michel-
angelo carried it no further than a finished drawing." See
also A. Springer, " Raffael und Michelangelo," vol. ii.,
pp. 306—311.

spoke of adding goodness to things already perfect so as to win more experience by them, and I have seen ' omnia possibilia sunt credenti.' I had a profound belief that God would grant you a supernatural faith to paint this Christ: and I found it so admirable as to exceed all that I had been able to imagine : and animated by your miracles, I wished for that which I now see miraculously fulfilled, that is, that it should be perfect in every respect, more could not be desired or even hoped for : I must tell you that I rejoice that the Angel on the right hand is so beautiful, for the Archangel Michael will place you, Michelangelo, on the right hand of the Lord on that new day. Meanwhile I do not know how to serve you better, than to pray to this sweet Christ for you, whom you have so well, so perfectly painted, and to beseech you that you may command me as altogether yours in all things." Another of her letters speaks in more familiar tones, and shows the pleasant relationship that existed between them :—
" Most sincere friend, Signore Michelagniolo, I beseech of you to send me for awhile the

crucifix, even if it is unfinished, for I would desire to show it to some gentlemen, who are come from the Most Reverend the Cardinal of Mantua. If you are not at work to-day, you might come at your leisure, and talk to me.

"Yours to command,

"LA MARCHESA DI PESCARA."

Only two of her sonnets are addressed to him, and both refer to some work he was engaged in on her behalf. The letters addressed to her by Michelangelo are of a later date, and were written when Vittoria had to retire from Rome under the suspicion of heresy, which her intercourse and friendship with Ochino drew upon her.

Society at this moment in Rome was in an unsettled state. From three different directions, from Venice, from Geneva, and from Naples, thoughts of a new and disturbing element were pouring into the capital of the world, and awakening discussion and division. The opinions from Venice and Geneva were soon put down with a high hand, as savouring of heresy. That

Naples should advocate such tendencies was
not, however, considered possible, and in con-
sequence, the Neapolitan movement was at this
moment occupying all thoughtful minds in
Rome. At the head of this movement was
Ochino, and the endeavour of his party was to
place the Lutherans on a better footing with
the Pope, and to bring about a peaceful agree-
ment between the opponents. On the other
side was the order of the Theatines, who were
zealous to reform the Church from within, and
to effect a renovation which should restore her
to her earlier purity, without causing a division
such as had arisen in Germany. This order
took their name from Pietro Caraffa, Bishop of
Theate, a "lean and impetuous Neapolitan,
with the fierceness of the Inquisition in his
heart,"[4] who afterwards became Pope under the
name of Paul IV.

Rome was thus divided between these two
parties; the one, that of Caraffa, defying the
Protestants, and asserting a crusade of uncom-

---

[4] "Venetian Studies." F. Horatio Brown.

promising antagonism against them; the other, to which Ochino belonged, and in which he had the support of Vittoria Colonna, Cardinals Contarini, Pole, and Sadoleto, which strove, by toleration and patience, to win the lost sheep back to the fold. The charge of heresy which Ochino's more liberal views drew down upon himself, fell also on his companions. Vittoria did not escape from the imputation, and we shall presently see how her intercourse with Michelangelo was interrupted for some time in consequence of this accusation.

Before this took place, however, it may be well to give a description that has come down to us from a certain Francesco d'Ollanda, of the friendly relations between Vittoria and Michelangelo. Francesco was a miniature painter, in the service of the King of Portugal, by whom he had been sent to Italy to study his art. He describes two Sunday afternoons that he spent in the company of Vittoria Colonna; Claudio Tolomei, one of the noblest and most distinguished of the literary men at that time in Rome; Ochino and Michelangelo. Francesco d'Ollanda's manuscript, preserved in the library at Lisbon, has been partly translated into French by Count Raczynsky.[5] The graphic, minute rendering of the scene must excuse its length. He explains first how his time in Rome was devoted to art, and in search of the men who would help him in respect of it; how his habit was to pass his Sundays with " Messer Tolomei," and how, on this particular Sunday, Tolomei had bidden him join him at the Church of San Silvestro, where he would also find the Marchesa di Pescara, and where an exposition of St. Paul's Epistles was being given by Ochino. A full panegyric then follows on the Marchesa di Pescara, her beauty, her goodness, her talents, and then he joins the party at San Silvestro.

" I entered: they asked me to take a place, and the reading and exposition of the epistles was continued. When it was ended the Marchesa spoke, and, looking at me and Tolomei, she said, ' I am not quite wrong if I imagine

---

[5] Raczynsky, " Les Arts en Portugal." 8vo. Paris, 1846.

that Messer Francesco would rather listen to Michelangelo upon painting than Fra Ambrosio upon the Pauline Epistles.'

" ' Madam,' I replied, ' your Excellence seems to entertain the belief that everything which is not painting and art is foreign and unintelligible to me. It will be certainly very agreeable to me to hear Michelangelo speak, but I prefer Fra Ambrosio's expositions of the epistles of St. Paul.' I had spoken somewhat in pique.

" ' You need not take it so seriously,' interrupted Tolomei; ' the Marchesa certainly did not mean that a man, who is a good painter, is not good for anything else. We Italians rank art too high for that. Perhaps the words of the Marchesa were intended to intimate that, besides the enjoyment we have had, the other, of hearing Michelangelo speak to-day, is still in store for us.'

" ' If it be so,' I replied, ' it would, after all, be nothing extraordinary, for your Excellency would only be following your usual habit of granting a thousand times more than one ventured to desire.'

" The Marchesa smiled. 'We ought to know how to give,' she said, 'when a grateful mind is concerned, and here, especially, when giving and receiving afford equal enjoyment.' One of her retinue had approached at her call. 'Do you know Michelangelo's dwelling? Go and tell him that Messer Tolomei and I are here in the chapel, where it is beautifully cool, the church, too, is private and agreeable, and that I beg to ask whether he is inclined to lose a few hours here in our society, and to turn them into gain for us. But not a word that the gentleman from Spain is here.'

" I could not refrain from remarking, in a loud tone to Tolomei, with what art the Marchesa knew how to treat the slightest thing. She inquired what we were saying. 'Oh!' answered Tolomei, 'he said with what wisdom your Excellency went to work even in so trifling a message. For, as Michelangelo knows that when he once meets Messer Francesco, there is no possibility of separating, he avoids him whenever he can.'

" 'I have remarked it,' said the Marchesa;

'I know Michelangelo. But it will be diffi-
cult to bring him to speak upon painting.'

" Fra Ambrosio [6] of Siena, one of the Pope's
most famous preachers, had hitherto not uttered
a syllable. 'As the gentleman from Spain,'
he now began, 'is himself a painter, Michel-
angelo will be cautious of speaking of painting.
The gentleman ought to conceal himself if he
wishes to hear him speak about it.'

" ' It would, perhaps, be more difficult than
you imagine to keep the gentleman from Spain
concealed from Michelangelo,' I replied, with
some severity, to the reverend gentleman;
'even if I were concealed, he would observe
my presence sooner than your reverence would
were I not concealed, though you took
spectacles to help you. Only let him come,
whether he remarks that I am here or no.'

" The Marchesa and Tolomei laughed. After
some moments, in which neither of them spoke,
we heard knocking at the door. Every one

---

[6] Ochino, or Fra Bernardino of Siena, was often called
Fra Ambrosio.

feared it could not be Michelangelo, who lived down below on Monte Cavallo. The servant had met him; he fell at once into the snare, and it was he who now knocked at the door.

"The Marchesa rose to receive him, and remained standing some time, until she had made him take a place between herself and Tolomei. I seated myself at some little distance from them. At first they were silent; then, the Marchesa, who could never speak without elevating those with whom she conversed, and even the place where she was, began to lead the conversation with the greatest art upon all possible things, without, however, touching even remotely upon painting. She wished to give Michelangelo confidence. She proceeded, as if approaching an unassailable fortress, so long as he was on his guard. But at last he yielded.

"'It is an old experience,' she said, 'that no one can rise against Michelangelo, who would contend against him with his own weapons, that is, with mind and art. And so you will see, there is only one means of having the last word with him, and that is, to speak of law-suits or painting, and he will not say a word more.'

" 'Or rather, I now remarked from my corner,' 'the best means of wearying Michelangelo out, would be simply to let him know I am here, for he has not seen me up to this moment. Of course the surest means of concealing from him anything so unimportant as I am was to come close under his eyes.'

" ' Pardon, Messer Francesco,' he called out, turning with astonishment towards me, ' it was impossible to see you—I saw no one here but the Marchesa. But since you are providentially there, come as a colleague to my help.'

" ' The Marchesa,' I replied, ' seems, like the sun, to show things to one, but to dazzle another, who looks at her. With you, she is to blame that you have not seen me, and with me she is the cause of my seeing you at all to-day. Who moreover,' I added, ' in discussion with her Excellency would have any thoughts left for his neighbour? He needs them truly for himself, and for this reason alone,' I concluded, turning to Fra Ambrosio, ' it seemed to me superfluous till now to follow the good counsel of a certain reverend gentleman.'

"All laughed. Fra Ambrosio rose, took his leave of the Marchesa, greeted us, and left. He has since been among my best friends.

"' His Holiness,' said the Marchesa, again renewing the conversation, ' has had the goodness to grant me permission to build a new convent in this immediate neighbourhood, half way up Monte Cavallo, where the tower stands from which Nero looked down on the burning city. The footsteps of pious women are to efface the traces of the wicked. I don't know, Michelangelo, how I shall have the building erected, how large, and facing which side. The old wall, perhaps, might be still employed.'

"' Certainly,' he replied ; ' the old tower might hold the bells. I see no difficulty in this building. We would, if your Excellency likes, take a view of the place on the way home.'

" 'I had not ventured to ask this,' answered she, ' but I see the words of our Lord, " Every one that humbleth himself shall be exalted," are true under all circumstances. But you understand how to give conscientiously where others only lavish at 'random, and therefore your friends rank yourself so much higher than your works, and those who only know your works, and not yourself, value that in you which can only be called perfect on a lower scale. I cannot but admire the manner in which you withdraw yourself from the world, from useless conversation, and from all the offers of princes, who desire paintings from your hand—how you avoid it all, and how you have disposed the labour of your life as one single great work.'

" 'Gracious lady,' replied Michelangelo, ' these are undeserved praises, but as the conversation has taken this turn, I must here complain of the public.'

" After this the conversation became general, painting still continuing the topic, till finally Messer Francesco finished an encomium on Italy

G

and the art contained in it by saying, 'Among so many princes and nobles, one alone, however, has gained the surname of the divine— one painter only, and that is Michelangelo!'

"'You speak like a good Italian, and as if you had been born among us,' said the Marchesa, as I finished. And then she began a eulogium about painting; she spoke of its ennobling influence upon a people; how it led them to piety, to glory, to greatness, until the tears came into her eyes from the emotion within. Thus passed the time. It had become late. Michelangelo first rose. The Marchesa stood up. I begged her to grant me the happiness of being allowed to appear at this reunion again on the following Sunday She acceded to my request, and Michelangelo promised to come. We accompanied them to the gates. Tolomei went with Michelangelo, and I with the Marchesa, from San Silvestro up to the monastery where the head of St. John the Baptist is preserved, and where she lived. From there I set out on the way home."

The next Sunday's meeting is not related,

but Vittoria was absent from it. She granted, however, a special audience to Francesco, but the account of this has not come down to us.

From the time when Vittoria and Michelangelo first met, their intercourse and friendship had gone on with increasing and elevating vigour ; and these years may assuredly be looked upon as the happiest in the whole of Michelangelo's long life. Then came the revolution of 1541, and all was changed. The party to which Vittoria belonged, and whose success at one moment appeared certain, failed in their efforts. The ' via media ' which they had striven for, had only brought suspicion upon them from the Lutherans, and accusations of heresy from Caraffa and his followers. Caraffa was now all-powerful in Rome, and consequently his opponents could no longer find a home there. Contarini and Pole had both left Rome, and Vittoria determined to follow the latter to Viterbo.[7] Here she lodged

---

[7] Cardinal Reginald Pole was born in March, 1500, in the county of Stafford. He became, in turn, Archbishop of Canterbury and Apostolic Legate in England. On com-

in the convent of Sta. Caterina, and endea-
voured to gather round her some of her old
friends, no longer though in the close and
familiar intercourse of former days. That was
over and past, and her aim was only to escape
unnoticed from the hostility of those attacks
which pursued her even in her retreat.

In the following year that circle of friends
was narrowed by the death of " the learned and
saint-like Venetian," Cardinal Contarini,[8] and

---

pleting his studies at Oxford he went to Italy, and passed
five years at Padua; and after visiting the chief towns in
Italy he returned to England. He chose exile rather than
submit to Henry VIII.'s declaration of himself as head of
the English Church; and he further incurred his royal
cousin's displeasure on the question of Henry's divorce
with Katharine of Aragon. He took refuge in Italy, and
on refusing to change his opinions as to the King's marriage,
Henry deprived him of his livings and emoluments. To
compensate him for his losses, Paul III. raised him to the
cardinalate, and sent him as Papal Legate to France, and
afterwards to Flanders. The remainder of his life was spent
for the most part at Viterbo.

[8] Contarini died in August, 1542, at Bologna, of which
town he was governor. He was a Venetian senator, held
in high esteem by Charles V., and beloved by all who knew
him for his frankness, goodness, and true nobility of cha-
racter. He was renowned, too, for learning, for his interest
in philosophy, and was a most diligent student of Aristotle.

we give the sonnet which Vittoria wrote on this occasion, and sent with a long letter of condolence to his sister. In this sonnet she says how Contarini should have been made Pope to render the age happy.

Scarce do I see far off some tiny spray
Of budding hope appear, some flower unclose
Potent to stay our tears, to soothe our woes,
But envious Death straight snatcheth it away.
The noble spirit that from mortal clay
Set free, on safer shore now seeks repose,
To our loved land, triumphant o'er her foes,
Might have fulfill'd the so much sighed-for day,

And Tiber's ancient glories brought again;
For had the fit reward his toils repaid,
With every grace and every virtue crown'd,

---

[9] Non prima e da lontan picciola fronde
  Scorgo di verde speme, nè si viva
  Che agli occhi il pianto, e 'l duol al cor prescriva,
  Ch' invida morte subito l' asconde.
  Potean le grazie e le virtù profonde
  Dell' alma bella, di vil core schiva
  Ch' or prese il volo a più sicura riva,
  Vincendo queste irate e torbid' onde

  Rendere al Tebro ogni sua gloria antica;
  E all' alma patria di trionfi ornata
  Recar quel tanto sospirato giorno

Passing securely o'er the angry main,
This age of ours he happy might have made
By Peter's mighty mantle compass'd round.

Another blow fell on her and on Pole in the fact of Ochino's full avowal of Luther's doctrines. Vittoria had upheld him to the utmost, and in consequence the supervision kept over her by the Inquisition was of the strictest. She had to submit to the ruling powers, and Ochino's apology, written to her at Viterbo as to an old friend, she deemed prudent to send to the authorities in Rome.

While absent from Rome she wrote often to Michelangelo, and he on his part wrote so frequently that she checked his too-fluent pen in these words: " Should you continue our correspondence with such ardour, you will cause me to miss attending the service with the sisters in the chapel of St. Catherine of an evening, and yourself from starting early to work at St. Peter's. And in this case, one will

---

Che, pareggiando il merto alla fatica,
  Facesse questa età nostra beata
  Del gran manto di Pier coperta intorno.

be wanting towards the brides of Christ, and the other towards his vicar." [1]

She was also in the habit of sending him any of her new writings, which he had bound up in a volume of her poems which she had presented to him when departing for Viterbo. It would appear to be this to which he refers in the second of the sonnets he addressed to her, the translation of which is as follows ·[2]—

Seeking at least to be not all unfit
For thy sublime and boundless courtesy,
My lowly thoughts at first were fain to try
What they could yield for grace so infinite.
But now I know my unassisted wit
Is all too weak to make me soar so high ;

---

[1] " Che volendo continuarla con tanto calore, essa mancherebbe di stare la sera con le suore nella cappella di Sta. Caterina, ed egli di andare di buon' ora a lavorare a San Pietro ; e così l'una mancherebbe alle spose di Cristo, e l' altro al vicario."

[2] By kind permission of Mr. Symonds.

[3] Per esser manco almen, signioria, indegnio
  Dell' immensa vostr' alta cortesia,
  Prima, all' incontro a quella, usar la mia
 Con tutto il cor volse 'l mie basso ingegnio.
  Ma vista poi c' ascendere a quel seguio
  Proprio valor non è c' apra la via,

For pardon, lady, for this fault I cry,
And wiser still I grow remembering it.

Yea, well I see what folly 'twere to think
That largess dropp'd from thee like dews from
　　heaven
Could e'er be paid by work so frail as mine !
To nothingness my art and talent sink ;
He fails who from his mortal stores hath given
A thousandfold to match one gift divine.

Her writings were eagerly looked for and read in Italy. The first edition was published during her lifetime, and without her knowledge, at Parma, in 1538. Five editions followed in ten years, and the demand for fresh publications still continued.

---

Perdon domanda la mia colpa ria,
　　E del fallir più saggio ognior divegnio.

E veggio ben com' erra, s 'alcun crede
　　La grazia, che da voi divina piove,
　　Pareggi l' opra mia caduca e frale.
L' ingegnio e l' arte e la memoria cede ;
　　C' un don celeste mai con mille pruove
　　Pagar può sol del suo chi è mortale.*

* "Le Rime di Michelangelo Buonarotti, cavate dagli autographi e pubblicate da Cesare Guasti." Firenze, 1863.

Towards the close of this year Vittoria left Viterbo, and returned to Rome, where her meeting with Michelangelo must have been a sad one. She had gone through a severe illness, and came with shattered health and spirits prostrated by the ruin of her family, for though a real and humble servant of God and the Church, she remained to the last a Colonna, a daughter of one of the first and proudest families of Italy. That family were at this moment far from prosperous. Paul III. had deprived Ascanio of most of his territories, and the Papal War against the Colonna in 1541, had been entirely to the advantage of the Pope. Vittoria addressed a sonnet to Paul, in which she endeavours to instil milder thoughts in the mind of the Pontiff.

[4] My country's open plains gleam on my view
With war o'erspread. Laughter is turn'd to woe,
And happy song to cadence sad and slow
There where the earliest breath of life I drew.

---

[4] Veggio rilucer sol di armate squadre
I miei sì larghi campi, ed odo il canto
Rivolto in grido e 'l dolce riso in pianto
Là 've io prima toccai l' antica madre.

By noble deeds, cause that thy heart anew
With mild desires, O shepherd wise, may flow,
Thy sacerdotal robe put on to show
Thyself the first Pope's own successor true.

If wrath does not conceal the truth from thee,
We 'mongst your oldest sons may claim a place,
And for our worth were wont beloved to be.
Born of one womb, 'neath one sky's starry space,
Under the self-same city's pleasant shade
Our common ancestors one home have màde.

Vittoria found none of her kinsfolk in Rome,
and so retired to the convent of St. Anna
de' Fumari (now de' Falegnami), and here,
says Visconti, "In religious silence, absorbed
more than ever in contemplation of divine

---

Deh, mostrate con l' opre alte e leggiadre
　　Le voglie umili, o pastor saggio e santo !
　　Vestite il sacro glorïoso manto,
　　Come buon successor del primo padre.

Semo, se 'l vero in voi non copre o adombra
　　Lo sdegno, pur di quei più antichi vostri
　　Figli, è da' buoni per lungo uso amati !
Sotto un sol cielo, entro un sol grembo nati
　　Sono e nudriti insieme alla dolce ombra
　　D' una sola città gli avoli nostri.

sweetness, she composed her last poems, which breathe truly an air of blessed happiness." The last years of her life were passed in this convent, and during this time were composed the greater part of the " Rime Sacre e Morali."

Her health, which had been failing for some time, received a cruel shock in the death of her adopted son the Marchese del Vasto.[5] This happened in March, 1546. The Marchese had been appointed to the command of the infantry on that ill-advised expedition which Charles V led in person into Africa, and there, in the flower of his age, he died. Vittoria wrote the following sonnet on his death, and we seem to trace her prostration of mind and body in the less poetic rendering of the sonnet :—

[6] If your own mother true, my Lord and Son,
   A captive lived, from her would not be ta'en

---

[5] According to Brantome, the Marchese del Vasto was : " A handsome man, and exceeding gallant ; very particular as to dress, and, whether at peace or at war, made so strong a use of perfumes that even his horse's saddle smelt of essences."

[6] Figlio e signor, se la tua prima e vera
   Madre vive prigion, non l' è già tolto

Her soul and spirit wise, and in their train
Th' unconquered host of virtues every one.
But I, who with such links for aye have done,
While earth's most narrow plot does now retain
My heart, I crave a glance from thee again,
Lest thy new mother should by death be won.

Thou in the spacious fields of heaven dost now
In glory walk ; no darkness there can be,
To hinder or retard thy speedy race.
Old and enfeebled am I grown.  Do thou,
Who art with heavenly radiance fill'd, for me
Humbly implore th' Eternal Father's grace.

Her health was most seriously affected by
this blow, and early in the next year she was
removed in an almost dying condition from the

---

L' anima saggia, o 'l chiaro spirto sciolto,
Nè di tante virtù l' invitta schiera.
A me, che sembro andar scarca e leggiera
E'n poca terra ho il cor chiuso e sepolto,
Convien ch' abbi talor l' occhio rivolto,
Chè la novella tua madre non pèra.

Tu par gli aperti spaziosi campi
Del ciel cammini, e non più nebbia o pietra
Ritarda o ingombra il tuo spedito corso.
Io grave d' anni agghiaccio.  Or tu ch' avvampi
D' alma fiamma celeste, umil m' impetra
Dal comun Padre eterno omai soccorso.·

convent to the palace of Giuliano Cesarini, husband of Giulia Colonna, and the only one of her family then in Rome. Cardinal Pole, whom she had named as one of her executors, had been sent for, but before he came, she breathed her last on the 25th February, 1547.

Michelangelo saw her up to the last, and was so affected by her death, that, as Condivi relates, he nearly lost his senses. (Per la costei morte più se ne stette sbigottito e come insensato.) The last thing he had drawn for her was a Madonna, sitting at the foot of the cross, while upon the triangle above it denoting the Trinity, were inscribed those words of Dante, " Non vi si pensa quanto sangue costa." [6] He composed four sonnets on her death, the first of which we select [7] :—

[9] When my rude hammer to the stubborn stone
Gives human shape, now that, now this, at will;

---

[7] " They think not there how much of blood it costs." Par. xxix. 91. Longfellow's translation.

[8] Mr. Symonds's translation.

[9] Se 'l mie rozzo martello i duri sassi
Forma d' uman aspetto or questo, or quello,

Following his hand who wields and guides it still,
It moves upon another's feet alone :
But that which dwells in Heaven, the world doth fill
With beauty by pure motions of its own ;
And since tools fashion tools which else were none,
Its life makes all that lives with living skill.

Now, for that every stroke excels the more
The higher at the forge it doth ascend,
Her soul that fashion'd mine hath sought the skies:
Wherefore unfinish'd I must meet my end,
If God, the great Artificer, denies
That aid which was unique on earth before.

As we have seen from Condivi, he went to
see her on her deathbed, and came away in
tears lamenting that he had only kissed her

---

Dal ministro, ch' el guida iscorgie e tiello,
    Prendendo il moto, va con gli altrui passi :
Ma quel divin, ch' in cielo alberga e stassi,
    Altri, e sè più, col proprio andar fa bello ;
    E se nessun martel senza martello
    Si può far, da quel vivo ogni altro fassi.

E perchè 'l colpo è di valor più pieno
    Quant' alza più se stesso alla fucina,
    Sopra 'l mie, questo a ciel n' è gito a volo.
Onde a me non finito verrà meno,
    S' or non gli dà la fabbrica divina
    Aiuto a farlo, c' al mondo era solo.

hand, and not her face and forehead as well. The only thought that consoled him was that his own career was near its close. He was seventy years old, and nothing could compensate for the loss of such a friend as Vittoria had been to him. Their lives had journeyed on through ten years together, and the experiences and troubles that befell him had been known and shared by her. So the darkness fell with redoubled gloom, and settled for ever on the waning days of his earthly life.

Vittoria appointed her brother Ascanio her chief heir; Cardinal Pole being, as we have said, one of the executors. In her will she provided for her servants. She bequeathed legacies of a thousand scudi [1] to the four convents which had sheltered her at different times, St. Anna and St. Silvestro in Rome, St. Paolo at Orvieto, and Sta. Caterina at Viterbo. To Cardinal Pole she left nine thousand scudi. [2] "Ita

---

[1] The Roman scudo was worth five francs.
[2] This legacy the "Cardinal of England," as he was styled by his contemporaries, Pole presented to Vittoria's niece, who was also called Vittoria. She was the daughter

testavi ego Vittoria Colonna," is written in her own hand at the end of this document. Her letters were always signed, "Marchesa di Pescara."

With meekness and humility she desired to be buried without pomp or ceremony, and directed only that her "funeral should be after the manner of those who die in convents." Her wishes were acceded to, and she was laid in the common burial-ground of the nuns of Sant' Anna. No stone points out the spot of her grave, and we may seek in vain for some record of her last resting-place. But an eternal monument exists for us in her poems and writings, and we can ask for no lovelier epitaph than the following sonnet, which sums up in touching words all that we owe to Vittoria Colonna :—

> " Serene, and sad, and still, she sat apart
>   In widow'd saintliness, an unvowed nun,
>   Whose duty to the world without was done ;
> And yet concealing with unselfish art

---

of Ascanio Colonna, and afterwards wife of Don Garzia di Toledo.

The scars of grief, the pangs of loss, the smart
Of pain, she suffer'd not herself to shun
The hurt, and bruised, and wrong'd, who one by
   one
Sought sanctuary of her cloister'd heart.

But to that loneliest soul who found in her
His type of womanhood, supremest set,
And knew not whether he should kneel or no,
Such sweet strange comfort did she minister,
That, were this deed her all, the world would yet
Have loved her for the love of Angelo ! "

# III.

THE " Rivista Moderna," for the year 1878, contains an article of Conte Giuseppe Campori's, in which, speaking of Vittoria Colonna's writings, he says, " that in order to form a fair judgment of her poetical merits, one must equally avoid the exaggerated praises of the ' litterati' of her age, and the severe criticism that has been passed in modern times. Not all her compositions," he goes on to say, " are first rate, some indeed do not rise above mediocrity, added to which, the want of variety is apt to engender weariness to the reader. On the other hand, the elegance of the versification, the delicacy, and sometimes the originality of ideas, the blending of passionate and melancholy sentiment in her poems, explain the esteem in which they were held by contemporaries, together with the frequent demands made for new editions. Of her prose compositions, two only are known to us, and are short works on religious subjects. Her letters are written in haste, without date, and, with few exceptions, without study or care.[1]

In order that the reader may form his own opinion on Vittoria's sonnets, I have endeavoured to give some of those which seem to justify Campori's judgment, for "elegance" and "delicacy of idea," but which were omitted from her history, as having no bearing on the events of her life. The influence exercised on her by Petrarch is visible in many of her sonnets, perhaps nowhere so strongly as in the following ·—

[2] How limpid were the waves, how smooth the sea,
What time my bark sped forth upon her way!
Within her hold what priceless treasures lay!
Pure was the air, the breezes follow'd free :

---

[1] "Atti e Memorie delle R. R. Deputazioni di Storia Patria, per le provincie dell' Emilia." Vol. iii. Parte Seconda. Modena, 1878.

[2] Oh che tranquillo mar, oh che chiare onde
Solcava già la mia spalmata barca,
Di ricca e nobil merce adorna e carca,
Con l' aer puro e con l' aure seconde!

Heaven that now hides her glorious lights from me
Serene and cloudless usher'd in the day.
Needs must he fear whose life's dawn breaks too gay :
Setting with rising seldom shall agree.

And lo! how Fortune, fickle and unkind,
A frowning, angry visage towards me shows,
Whose fury sets the elements at war ;
Lightnings she joins with rain and raging wind,
The monsters of the deep around me close :
Yet still my soul discerns the faithful star.

That Vittoria was also influenced by Dante is visible in some of her sonnets, and I have selected one which echoes almost the same words and ideas that Francesca da Rimini has made familiar to every reader of the Divine Comedy :—

---

Il ciel, ch' ora i bei vaghi lumi asconde,
Porgea serena luce e d' ombra scarca ;
Ahi quanto ha da temer chi lieto varca !
Chè non sempre al principio il fin risponde.

Ecco l' empia e volubile fortuna
Scoperse poi l' irata iniqua fronte,
Dal cui furor sì gran procella insorge.
Venti, pioggia, saette, insieme aduna,
E fiere intorno a divorarmi pronte :
Ma l' alma ancor la fida stella scorge.

What lofty aims, what dulcet thoughts and dear
Nourish'd in me that sun, that drove away
The gathering clouds, and radiant made the day
Which now where'er I turn shows dull and drear.
How grateful was the sigh, how sweet the tear
That came to me in this his transient stay;
For then his parlance wise, his aspect gay,
Solaced my hopes, and well-nigh quell'd my fear.

Quench'd now I see that valour, spent and dead
That genial worth, and in the common woe
Confused and sad the noblest minds are left.
For when from earth he pass'd, there with him fled
The high heroic aims of long ago ;
And of all good my spirit was bereft.

---

[3] Quanti dolci pensieri, alti disiri
    Nodriva in me quel sol che d' ogn' intorno
    Sgombrò le nubi, e fe' qui chiaro il giorno,
    Ch' or tenebroso scorgo ovunque io miri !
Soave il lagrimar, grati i sospiri
    Mi rese in questo suo breve soggiorno ;
    Chè al parlar saggio ed allo sguardo adorno
    S' acquetavano in parte i miei martiri.

Veggio or spento il valor, morte e smarrite
    L' alme virtuti, e le più nobil menti
    Per lo danno comun meste e confuse.
Al suo sparir dal mondo son fuggite
    Di quel' antico onor le voglie ardenti,
    E le mie d' ogni ben per sempre escluse.

" Her sonnets," says Symonds, " penetrated
by genuine feeling, and almost wholly free
from literary affectation, have that dignity and
sweetness which belong to the spontaneous
utterance of a noble heart." And he further
goes on to say, how those of a religious
character " have in general the same simplicity
and sincerity of style." [4] In some of them the
proof of her Romanism is clearly set forth by
her invocation of the Madonna and St. Francis;
in others again (and of these I add two
examples) she turns to the cross of Christ with
all the fervour of deep piety :—

[5] When on my many sins I gaze intent,
  From God the Father then my face I hide
  In shame, and unto Thee, who for us died
  On cross of Calvary, my heart is bent.
  Thy love and wounds to me a shield have lent
  To turn all past and present wrath aside.

---

[4] " Italian Literature."   Chap. xiii., pp. 294, 295.
[5] Quand' io riguardo il mio sì grave errore,
  Confusa al Padre Eterno il volto indegno
  Non ergo allor, ma a te, che sovra il legno
  Per noi moristi, volgo il fedel core.
  Scudo delle tue piaghe e del tuo amore
  Mi fo contra l' antico e novo sdegno.

Thou art to me a sure and precious guide,
Who our deep woes hast turn'd to glad content.

For us Thou didst entreat in death's dread hour
Saying, " I would, O Father, that above
Be those who trust in Me."   Whence my soul free
From earthly fears acknowledges the power
Of that pure zeal, which led Thee in Thy love
To crucify my sins upon Thy tree.

Sometimes our thoughts are bent on the great Son
Upon the cross, by faith inspired, whence light
Calm and serene streams down in radiance bright,
Leading them glorious to th' Almighty's throne.

Tu sei mio vero prezïoso pegno,
Che volgi in speme e gioia, ansia e timore.

Per noi su l' ore estreme umil pregasti,
Dicendo : Io voglio, o Padre, unito in cielo
Chi crede in me, sì ch' or l' alma non teme.
Crede ella e scorge tua mercè, quel zelo
Del quale ardesti sì, che consumasti
Te stesso in croce e le mie colpe insieme.

Vanno i pensier talor carchi di vera
Fede al gran Figlio in croce ; ed indi quella
Luce, ch' ei porge lor serena e bella,
Gli guida al Padre in gloriosa schiera.

Now in the faithful soul, this favour done
Will cause no pride to dwell, who has in fight
Prevail'd, putting the world and self to flight,
But all the honour gives to God alone.

No wings unwafted by celestial wind
Can reach those far-off heights, no eye avail
To see the upward path without Heaven's ray.
Our works are vain, and all our wills are blind
At the first flight our mortal pinions fail,
Unless in Christ we find our help and stay.

The following sonnet will serve as an example
of Vittoria's lighter style, with greater play of
fancy than in the foregoing ones :—

[6] The hungry nestling when he sees and hears
His mother's wings beat round him as she flies

---

Nè quest' almo favor rende più altera
L' alma fedel, poichè fatta è rubella
Del mondo e di sè stessa, anzi rende ella
A Dio dell' onor suo la gloria intera.

Non giungon l' umane ali all' alto segno
Senza il vento divin, nè l' occhio scopre
Il bel destro sentier senza 'l gran lume.
Cieco è 'l nostro voler, vane son l' opre,
Cadono al primo vol le mortal piume
Senza quel di Gesù fermo sostegno.

---

• Qual digiuno augellin, che vede ed ode
Batter l' ali alla madre intorno, quando

To fetch him food, with glad and eager eyes
Welcomes her coming and the gift she bears ;
And to requite her for her tender cares,
Flapping and fluttering round the nest, he tries
To join her flight ; his tongue he then unties
And bursting into song his love declares.

So I, what time the warm and quickening ray
Of that fair sun, whereon my life is fed,
With more than wonted brightness on me shines,
Lost in delight, scarce knowing what I say,
With trembling pen by inward love am led
To write his praises in my faltering lines.

The following three sonnets, though not of
uch grace as some others by Vittoria, are of

---

Gli reca il nutrimento, ond' egli, amando
  Il cibo e quella, si rallegra e gode,
E dentro al nido suo si strugge e rode
  Per desio di seguirla anch' ei volando,
  E la ringrazia in tal modo cantando
  Che par ch' oltre 'l poter la lingua snode ;

Tal io qualor il caldo raggio e vivo
  Del divin sole, onde nutrisco il core,
  Più dell' usato lucido lampeggia,
Muovo la penna spinta dall' amore
  Interno ; e senza ch' io stessa m' avveggia
  Di quel ch' io dico, le sue lodi scrivo

interest as being now published for the first
time.[7]

8　Almighty Lord, whose loving care would show
　To us the load of sin and all its stain ;
　Whilst Thy blest zeal, which doth dispel our vain
　Desires, and unto us would grace bestow
　So full and free that every soul below
　Self-honouring, Thy worship might attain
　In purest faith.　O gentle Sun, maintain
　And succour this my soul by sin brought low.

　And though my sins in youth I do confess
　Have countless been, and in the days of old
　The time misspent has caused Thee sore distress,

---

　[1] I owe these sonnets to the researches of Signor Pro-
fessore Wiel, and they are to be found in the Marciana
Codice CCC., Class IX., in the Appendix of the Italian
Catalogue, Venice.

　　[8] Alto Signor, la cui picta m' insegna
　　　　Quanto de' nostri error gl' incresce (*sic !*) e dole,
　　　　Mentre il tuo santo ardor, per ch' ogni fole
　　　　Pensier lasciam, c' infondi ch' in noi vegna
　　Quella bontà, ch' ogni alma di se degna
　　　　Fece ch' il tuo bel nome onora, e cole
　　　　Con pura fede : o chiaro almo mio sole,
　　　　Questa mia peccatrice erga e sostegna.

　　E quantunque infinite, ch' io nol nego
　　　　Fosser le giovanil mie colpe, e tanto
　　　　T' offendesser gli già mal spesi giorni ;

May'st Thou in pardoning love our guilt enfold ;
Whilst I implore in penitence and tears
Thy grace to find Thee in my better years.

------

### 9 On the Death of Sannazzaro.

If in that age so wondrous and so fair,
Named for its worth the century of gold,
Virgil was born, and all that happy fold
Of souls, in glory wrapt and freed from care
The stars have given, in courteous grace to share,
To us Sannazzaro ; whose matchless, bold,
And varied style, excels all those of old
Who on their foreheads did the laurel wear.


Tu che sì a' nostri error sei facil, priego
   Mi dona, ond' io contrita in doglia, in pianto,
   Almen nei miglior anni a te ritorni.

------

### 9 Nella Morte del Sannazzaro.

Se a quella gloriosa e bella etade
   Che 'l nome meritò del secol d' oro
   Nacque Virgiliô, e quel sacrato coro
   Di tante altre felici alme beate,
Dato han le stelle a noi cortes' e grate
   L' unico Sannazzaro, il cui sonoro
   Leggiadro stil vince chi mai d' alloro
   Fu degno aver ambe le tempie ornate.

Death has removed him hence, and envious heaven
Adorned by him, is glad that to the state
Where Virgil has attain'd, he now is even.
This one his native town and stream made great,
And Naples by that other gains to fame;
While Sebeto will sing his deathless name.

---

### [1] TO THE DUKE OF MANTUA.

The Muses seek for wreaths of laurel bright,
And Helicon in hues of richest dyes
Apollo gilds, whilst flowers in sweet supplies
Life-giving Flora spreads on every height
For you, my lord; so 'mid those minds of might
For whose renown with us Parnassus vies,

Morte l' ha tolto poi, e 'l cielo avaro
   Di lui s' adorna, ma piu ch' altro lieto,
   Gode in vedersi al gran Virgilio eguale.
Quel Mantoa illustra, e fa 'l suo Mincio chiaro;
   Questi Napoli onora, e il bel Sebeto
   Farà non men famoso ed immortale.

---

### [1] AL DUCA DI MANTOVA.

Cercan le Muse i più pregiati allori,
   Orna Apollo Elicona e l' incolora
   Delle più rare gemme, e l' alma Flora
   Apre d' intorno ai monti i più bei fiori
Per voi, Signor, poi tra quei grandi autori
   Di cui Parnasso e nostra età si onori,

Like to Aurora flashing through dark skies,
Our glorious heroes shine with lasting light.

So ere you quit this earth a double crown
Shall deck your brow, and unto you belong
A twofold gift of glory and renown ;
Fame, both in war, and history's bright song
Shall be your meed ; so that my sun on high
Will hear your praises reach the starry sky.

The following translation of Ariosto's[2] praises of Vittoria (to which allusion has been made at page 57) is that of Sir John Harington, from the folio edition, London, 1634 :—

Shall I then all omit? that were not well,
Sith that to please them all I do desire :
Then will I chuse some one, that doth excell
The rest so farre, as none may dare envie her ;

---

Come nel ciel oscur fulge l' Aurora,
Lampeggian nostri illustri eterni onori.

Del gemino valor perpetua gloria
Vi veggio aver, e pria di cangiar pelo
D' ambe corone ornar la tempie belle
E or la spada, or lo stil di chiara istoria
Vi faran degno, onde 'l mio sole 'n cielo
Sente che 'l vostro onor giugne alle stelle.

"Orlando Furioso," Canto xxxvii. stanzas 16—20 (in the translation 10—14).

Whose name doth in such height of honour dwell,
As hard it is, for any to come nye her,
Whose learned pen such priviledge can give,
As it can make e'en those are dead to live.

For e'en as Phebus shines on ev'rie star,
Yet on his sister caste his fairest light,
So eloquence and grace ay shining are,
Much more on her, than any other wight ;
And maketh her to passe the rest as farre,
As Phebe doth the other starrs in night,
Her light so splendent is, and so divine,
As makes another Sunne on earth to shine.

Vittoria is her name, a most fit name,
For one in triumphs borne, in triumphs bred,
That passeth Artimesia in the fame
Of doing honour to her husband ded ;
For though she did erect a wondrous frame,
For her Mausolio, with a Pyramed,
Yet which is more, to lay the dead in grave
Or else from death, with learned pen to save.

If Laodamia, and if Brutus' wife,
Argia, Arria, and Evadne chaste,
Be to be praised, as they are so rife,
Because when as their husbands' dayes were past,
They willingly forsooke this mortall life :
Then in what height must she of right be plast ?
That such a gift unto her spouse doth give,
That being dead, she still doth make him live.

And if the great Macedon envie bare
Unto Achilles, for Meonian Lyré,
Much more to noble Francis of Pescara,
He would have.borne, whose praise is founded hyre
By such a wife, so virtuous, chast, and rare
As ev'n thy soule itselfe could not desire
A louder trumpe thy praises out to sound,
Sith hardly can a match to this be found.

# APPENDIX.

Lettera dell' Imperatore Carlo V. alla Signora Vittoria Colonna, Marchesa di Pescara, per congratularsi della vittoria riportata dal marito alla battaglia di Pavia (24 febbo., 1525) colla risposta della sudditta Marchesa all' Imperatore.[1]

*Estratto dal volume 38 dei Diarii autografi di Marin Sanuto esistenti nella Biblioteca Marciana di Venezia.*

Sanuto Marino Diarii, vol. xxxviii., Co. 260.
31 Maggio, 1525.

*Exemplum litterarum Cesareæ Majestatis ad Illustrissimam Dominam Marchionissam Pischariæ et responsio præfatæ Marchionissæ.*

Illustris consanguinea nostra carissima, quum primum allatum nobis est de tam insigni tam memorabili victoria quam Deus Optimus Maximus in Insubria nobis adversus Gallos concedere dignatus est, certe preter alia multa quæ

---

[1] Published now for the first time.

jucundissima nobis in mentem veniebant fuit
nominis tui recordatio, quam quidem et non
parum auxit qui hic agit pro illustri Marchione
Tuo conjuge Franciscus Quiterius, convenienti
gratulationis tuo nomine functus effecit, Tuum
Victoriæ nomen auspicatissimum nobis semper
redderemus neque in merito cum ex eo genere
sis ex ea familia ex qua tam nos quam maiores
nostri non vulgaria quocumque tempore officia
reportarunt. Tali vero cum marito coniuncta
cuius virtute et re bellica industria atque felici
tate extimemus non minimam tantæ victoriæ
partem constitisse merito, itaque Victoriæ victoria
gratularis, ex qua intelligere potes tantum in te
amplitudinis tantum potentiæ et gloriæ redun-
dare et comode cum nihil tam magnum sit quod
Marchio ipse de nostra gratitudine et liberalitate
spectare non possit, tanti vero animum Tuum
atque observantia ut pene mariti Tui merita
tecum communia judicemus tibique ob id quan-
tum est debemus. Vale.

*A tergo :* Illustri Victoriæ Colonnæ Mar-
chionissæ Pischariæ consanguineæ nostræ
carissimæ.

## Answer of Letter from Vittoria Colonna to the Emperor Charles V., after the Battle of Pavia, 1525.

If our Lord God, in regard of the supreme merit of your Cesarean Majesty, deigned to raise you in such an exalted degree that mighty kings expect from you liberty, and are compelled to entreat mercy from you, what boldness should I not show in answering your most kindly letter, did it not create within me light to understand it, and a soul to deserve it. Nor would any one arrogate to himself the desire to serve you, from the need to acquire your favour, but rather to ascribe to you your due, since in you is the supreme summit of all perfection and virtue, where they shine so brilliantly, the whole world is bathed therein. In your goodness every hope is placed, and mortals can look for no higher sign. And since your worth and intelligence suffice in themselves to make you happy and blessed, one need implore only that you will vouchsafe your own greatness, the fruition of every satisfied will, which all the world owes to you, though it cannot give it. Taking your immense kindness as an acknowledged fact, a thing satisfactory to itself, and which supplying the wants of mankind will make you still more worthy of your noble empire.

But what shall I say of my happiness at having been in the memory of your Cesarean Majesty at a moment when you triumphed over so many nations, when you disposed of so many royal lives, divided kingdoms and provinces, and when the peace of all Christendom and the consequent ruin of the Infidels depended on your judgment?

I could not presume to think, but that in the same hour, you would show that you knew how to put down the haughty and exalt the lowly, nor could anything be found so great that would not seem small (compared) to the greatness of your soul, nor anything so minute that your humanity would not accept as large, following in this respect, as in others, that Lord whom you, more than others, represent.

The services, faith and sincerity of my Lord Marquis, and of my house I hold for such, that unworthy as they are, they should be acceptable to your Cesarean Majesty, and the promise given by you, I desire more as a proof of this than for my unusual cupidity, although your gratitude and liberality always precede every just demand. Nor do I know whether most to value or accept the reward from so great a Prince, or the glory for which you say you are endebted.

My name I hold in the greatest honour, it having been held as a fortunate omen by your Cesarean Majesty, nor had it been incongruously bestowed on me, as I have experienced in past victories obtained over myself.

Desiring that from such imminent and divers perils, my Lord Marquis should speedily serve your Majesty so as to bring you rest and quiet, I shall ever pray our Lord God for the health of your Cesarean Majesty, so necessary to all the world, and particularly to us, who by this light only are ruled and illuminated.

## RISPOSTA ALLA DITTA LETTERA.

Sel nostro Signor Dio rispettando al superno merito di Vostra Cesarea Maestà se degnò elevarla in si excelso grado che li potenti re ne aspettano libertà et sono costretti supplicarli mercede, che audacia teneria io de rispondere alla humanissima lettera se da essa medesima non nascesse in me luce per capirla et animo per meritarla, ne hoggi niuno può arrogarsi tanto che volendo servirla non gli bisogni col suo favore aquistare quanto ad essa vol restituire perchè ivi è il sommo columme de ogni perfectione, et virtuti si unite ivi rifulgeno che tutto il mondo ne resta nudato, in la sua bontà convien collocare ogni speranza che più alto segno non se concede a mortali, et perchè in la sola consideratione et intelligentia di se stessa è felice e beata, non convien supplicarli altro se non che poi se li concede la propria grandezza, la fruitione d'ogni desiderata voglia qual se deve tutto el mondo et non po darselo, tenerlo per la sua immensa benignitade per ricevuto, che cosi satisferà se stessa et supplendo

al mancamento dell' universo lo farà più merite-
vole del degno imperio suo. Ma che dirò de la
felicità mia, essendo stata ne la memoria de la
Vostra Cesarea Maestà in tempo che triumfava
de tanti nationi, disponea de le regie vite, repar-
tiva le provincie et regni, pendeva dal suo
judicio la quiete de tutta la Christianità et la
necessaria ruina de infedeli? Non presumerò
creder altro se non che in una medesma hora,
volesse mostrare che como sapeva debellare li
superbi, così sapea exaltare li humili, ni cosa
così grande po trovarse che alla magnitudine
del suo animo non sia piccola ne si minima che
la humanità sua non la ricevi per grande volendo
essere conforme in questo effetto come negli
altri a quel signore che più che mai altri facesse
rappresenta.

Li servicij fede et sincerità del marchese mio
signore, et de mia casa tengo per tali che
indegnamente sono a Vostra Cesarea Maestà
accetti, et la promessa, come dice, desidero più
per testimonio di questo che per insolità
cupidità mia, benchè la gratitudine et liberalità
sua, sempre previene ogni justa dimanda. Nè

so qual sia più da extimare o recevere il premio di tanto gran Principe, o la gloria che dica esserne debitore.

Il nome mio tengo in grandissima stima essendo da la Cesarea Maestà Vostra preso in augurio felice, nè incongruamente essendomi stà imposto per la vittoria de soi passati conosco haver solo in vincer me stessa usato. Desiderando più presto con tanti imminentissimi et diversi pericoli chel signor mio marchese servi sua Maestà che venga ad aquietarsi, come pregherò sempre nostro Signor Dio per la salute de la Cesarea Maestà Vostra, tanto necessaria a tutto el mondo, et precipue a noi che da solo questo lume siamo retti et illuminati.

THE END.

GILBERT AND RIVINGTON, LD., ST. JOHN'S HOUSE, CLERKENWELL ROAD, LONDON.

Printed in Great Britain
by Amazon

45173110R00076